90 0932548 9

GW00685211

The famous Brazilian educator Paulo Freire influenced educators, teachers and students in a broad tapestry of contexts and countries, as he challenged conventional thinking on how teachers ought to teach and learners ought to learn. By making his ideas accessible and relevant, this insightful and thought-provoking text draws out the relevance and topicality of Freire's work and applies this to a wide range of educational settings, from adult education, through schools, to early years settings.

Themes covered include:

- the lasting impact of illiteracy
- the benefits and potential in becoming literate
- literacy, language and power
- the differences between banking and dialogic education
- the social and political nature of learning
- what kind of teaching and learning do we want?

Using a variety of practical examples and case studies, *Introducing Freire* is an essential guide to the work of one of the most significant figures in education in the last century. Fascinating and accessible, this book is for anyone interested in teaching and learning, poverty and affluence, power and powerlessness, and society and change.

Sandra Smidt is a writer and consultant in early years education. She has previously written *The Developing Child in the 21ˢᵗ Century* (2013), *Introducing Malaguzzi* (2012), *Introducing Bruner* (2011), *Playing to Learn* (2010) and *Introducing Vygotsky* (2008), all published by Routledge.

Introducing Freire

A guide for students, teachers and practitioners

Sandra Smidt

Routledge
Taylor & Francis Group

LONDON AND NEW YORK

First published 2014
by Routledge
2 Park Square, Milton Park, Abingdon, Oxon OX14 4RN

and by Routledge
711 Third Avenue, New York, NY 10017

Routledge is an imprint of the Taylor & Francis Group, an informa business

© 2014 S. Smidt

The right of S. Smidt to be identified as author of this work has been asserted
by her in accordance with sections 77 and 78 of the Copyright, Designs and
Patents Act 1988.

All rights reserved. No part of this book may be reprinted or reproduced or
utilised in any form or by any electronic, mechanical, or other means, now
known or hereafter invented, including photocopying and recording, or in any
information storage or retrieval system, without permission in writing from
the publishers.

Trademark notice: Product or corporate names may be trademarks or
registered trademarks, and are used only for identification and explanation
without intent to infringe.

British Library Cataloguing in Publication Data
A catalogue record for this book is available from the British Library

Library of Congress Cataloging-in-Publication Data
Smidt, Sandra, 1943–
  Introducing Freire : a guide for students, teachers, and practitioners /
Sandra Smidt.
      pages cm
  1. Freire, Paulo, 1921–1997.   2. Education—Philosophy.   3. Literacy—
Social aspects.   I. Title.
    LB880.F732S65 2014
    370.1—dc23
    2013043289

ISBN: 978-0-415-71727-4 (hbk)
ISBN: 978-0-415-71728-1 (pbk)
ISBN: 978-1-315-77763-4 (ebk)

Typeset in Sabon
by Apex CoVantage, LLC

PLYMOUTH UNIVERSITY

9009325489

MIX
Paper from
responsible sources
FSC
www.fsc.org   FSC® C013056

Printed and bound in Great Britain by
TJ International Ltd, Padstow, Cornwall

Contents

Preface

When I was a very young woman in South Africa I got a part-time job working in an African night school. This was for black working people who had had little or no formal schooling. The students – all older than I was – came to the class after work. I had no training to teach but a growing political awareness of the effects of inequity. I hugely enjoyed the challenge and began to recognise two things: the first was how hard each student worked to complete the set work and the second how inappropriate to their needs the programme was. Only one example of just how inadequate to the needs of students such programmes can be remains in my memory. The students were asked to write an essay on 'the happiest day of my life'.

John wrote this: 'The best day of my life was when I asked my girlfriend to marry me and I osculated her reiteratedly'.

This, the fifth book in the *Introducing . . .* series takes a step sideways. All the other books in the series to date have focused on great thinkers in the field of early childhood development. This book examines the life, times and ideas of a great thinker whose work is firmly rooted in the world of adult education. As you read this book I hope you will begin to be able to make the links between the learning and development of young children and the learning and development of marginalised groups in society.

In October 1993 I was one of about 800 other people who gathered at the Institute of Education, in London, to listen to the words and ideas of the great Brazilian educator, Paulo Freire. Like many others I had read his best-known book *Pedagogy of the Oppressed* and when I heard he was to be leading a conference I did everything I could to be able to attend. The memory of it lives with me, of a quietly spoken man who, without any show or affectation, talked about his own life and experiences and how these had enabled him to determinedly set out to find the sources of oppression and examine the effects of this oppression on the life chances of men and women in his native country. As you read this book I hope something of his spirit emerges and you get the same sense I did, all those years ago, of someone who truly understood not only what it was like to be poor and denied access to questioning and challenging the world, but set out to find ways of changing this.

His approach to education was that it should be dialogic, which meant that he not only talked to the huge audience but listened to them. He was somehow able to turn a formal lecture into a more intimate dialogue and I left, at the end, with a sense of almost knowing him. It felt that we had touched minds.

Notes

1. In writing this book I will usually use the convention of 'she' rather than 'he' when writing about a nameless individual.
2. You will find some repetition in this book and this is because Freire's work is so wide-ranging and complex that he cannot talk about learning to read without being political or talk about oppression without considering literacy. His is a very political view which requires thinking about history, society, culture and much more.
3. He wrote in Portuguese and many of the earlier books are published without an index. Many of the Portuguese words are translated differently by different authors.
4. I will use UK spelling rather than the American spelling, which is often found in Freire's books which have all been translated from the Portuguese.
5. I will attempt to explain unfamiliar terms as they arise, but will also include them in a glossary at the end of the book.
6. Because this book is one in a series aimed primarily at those working with or interested in the learning and development of young children, in each chapter there may be a section looking at the implications for early childhood in the work and ideas of Paulo Freire. The sections will be in boxed and headed with the words *The intersection between the work of Paulo Freire and the world of early childhood development.*

Chapter 1

The life and times of Paulo Freire

In this chapter we look at the life of Paulo Freire and in doing that examine the events and people who influenced his thinking. Since he spent much of his life in exile we will move from Brazil to Chile to the United States of America to Switzerland and then back to Brazil after roughly seventeen years in exile.

The early years

Paulo Reglus Neves Freire, the youngest of the four children in the family, was born in the port of Recife, the capital of Pernambuco province in the northwest of Brazil in September 1921. His father, Joaquin Temistocles Freire, was an officer serving in the military police; his mother was Edeltrudes Neves Freire (referred to as Tudinha in some texts). She was a seamstress and ten years younger than her husband. The family was educated and described as being middle class. Freire himself said that his parents created a harmonious home atmosphere where it was possible to discuss and argue, show emotions and, as a Catholic family, live a life of religious belief. Paulo was very close to both his parents. His mother is said to have had enormous faith in him and in his intellect. His father would sing him to sleep and read him children's storybooks. With a real interest in his children's education he paved the way for Freire's later success.

Moacir Gadotti, in his idiosyncratic biography of Freire said that 'his chalk was the twigs of the mango tree in whose shade he learned to read, and his blackboard was the ground. This formation and information was all given informally, before school. It was a living, free, unpretentious preschool' (1994: 2). It was in this way that all four children were initiated into the world of reading by both parents: the mother teaching them to read by scratching letters and drawing pictures in the dusty ground of the yard of their house in the Yellow House District and the father telling stories and singing songs.

His first school was small and private and he could already write and copy and say the alphabet when he arrived there. What he never forgot was what he called 'making sentences'. This involved him in writing two or three words and then talking about them. The teacher clearly believed that hearing the words you have written said aloud and giving their meaning was a tool to becoming able to write expressively. You will see the significance of this later in the book. At this small school he was also introduced to many aspects of grammar which fascinated and intrigued him. His interest in linguistics and the rule-bound nature of language continued to fascinate him throughout his life. Until the year 1928 the family lived this pleasant middle-class life in their old house surrounded by trees and lush vegetation.

During the economic crisis of 1928–32, the Freire parents tried to uphold the standards of their middle-class life, but it became increasingly difficult for them to feed and clothe the family. When Paulo was ten years old they made the decision to move to the neighbouring city of Jaboatão, where life was less expensive. Here the family, like most others, experienced poverty with all its effects. Paulo soon became aware of the nature of the real world around him, encountering and befriending children living in extreme poverty. His own hunger pangs together with the other things he witnessed laid the foundations for his lifelong struggle against poverty and oppression. Tragically, two years after the move Joaquin died. Paulo was only thirteen years old at the time. With the trauma of moving home, experiencing poverty and the loss of his father he effectively lost two years of secondary schooling. But it seems that this was also a formative time. In her notes to Freire's *Pedagogy of Hope*, his second wife, Ana Maria, said:

> It was in Jaboatão where he lived from the age of eleven to twenty, that Paulo became acquainted with a world of difficulty, in which one lived on scant financial resources. There were difficulties arising from his mother's untimely widowhood, when society was much less open to a woman working outside the home than it is today. And there were the difficulties he felt personally, 'skinny, bony little kid' that he was, in fending off the hostility of a world that had such little sympathy for the weak and impoverished.
>
> But it was also in Jaboatão that he learned to play soccer . . . swam in the Jaboatão River, where he watched poor women, squatting and washing and beating against the rocks either their own families' clothes or those of more wealthy families, for whom they worked. It was there, again, that he learned to sing and whistle . . . and to dialogue in his 'circle of friends' . . . that he learned and assimilated – with a passion! – his

studies of both the popular and the cultivated syntax of the Portuguese language. (Ana Maria Araujo Freire in Freire 2009: 195)

It is reported by his few biographers that he was seen, at that time, as a failing student, with some of his teachers thinking that he had long-term developmental problems. In effect his problems with formal learning arose out of the traumas and crises he and his family endured in those years. So it is important here to reflect more deeply on the impact on him of moving from relative comfort and wealth at home to experiencing hunger, deprivation and educational failure. You will almost certainly know that what he is now famous for, throughout the world, is his outrage at how the poor are oppressed and kept silent so that the status quo is maintained. Drawn so directly from his own experience his working life was committed to understanding just what it was within educational establishments – classrooms, schools, universities and colleges – that ensured that the poor were kept ignorant, malleable and passive.

Brazil and beyond: into exile

After the death of her husband, Paulo's mother travelled daily from Jaboatão to Recife to try and get a scholarship for her beloved son. Early in 1937 she was successful and Paulo was enrolled at the prestigious private school *Ginasio Oswaldo Cruz* and became a highly successful pupil there. He later returned to the school as a teacher of Portuguese. When the economic crisis abated the family returned to its previous middle-class status. Paulo finished secondary schooling and went on to study law and philosophy at the University of Pernambuco.

You might want to know that Brazil has had, over time, the largest slave population in the world, substantially larger than that of the United States. The Portuguese who settled Brazil needed labour to work the large estates and mines in their new colony. They turned to slavery which became central to the colonial economy. It was particularly important in the mining and sugar cane sectors. It is concerning to note that today many employers in the country still subject employees to slave-like conditions. The government has what they call a "dirty list" – a list of those employers prepared to pay slave wages and impose terrible conditions on workers. The list was started in 2005 and is updated twice a year. There are now something like 294 employers, from big to small who happily uphold this practice. Brazil's legal category of what constitutes slave-like labour includes cases where a person may be subjected to exhausting hours, or forbidden to leave because of a debt with the employer and earns less than the minimum wage. Many cases of slave-like labour are found in rural areas where sugar cane and other crops are grown. Inspectors have also found workers submitted to slave-like conditions in the textile and clothing sector. It is certain that Freire encountered people living and working in slave-like conditions.

We come now to evidence of some of those who were influencing his thinking. Two of these were the lawyer and philosopher Rui Barbosa and the physician Carneiro Ribeiro, both of whom were celebrated Brazilian intellectuals. Barbosa was a political activist as well as a lawyer and gave his first public speech on the abolition of slavery when he was a mere nineteen-year-old. For the rest of his life he remained an uncompromising defender of civil liberties. Slavery in Brazil was only officially abolished in 1888. Part of Barbosa's legacy to history is that he authorised the destruction of most government records relating to slavery because he wanted to remove the stain of slavery from the communal memory. Less is known about Carneiro Ribeiro but we do know that he was a physician, a teacher and a linguist and we know that he wrote an important book on the Portuguese language, called *Serões Gramaticais*, sometimes translated as *Fireside Grammar*, or *Evening Grammar*. What is significant for us is that Ribeiro was working in a *sociolinguistic framework*, analysing how the Portuguese language developed over time and how important historical, social, political, economic and educational influences were and still are. As we will see this formed an essential grounding for what Freire later set out to do. As we look at some of the ways in which Freire worked in the early years to address the issues of illiteracy you will be able to trace his interest in grammatical features like the syllables that make up words to this influence.

Between 1944–5 Freire taught Portuguese language in Brazilian secondary schools: his law degree had qualified him to become a teacher. At the same time he worked as a trade union lawyer and lectured on legal matters to groups of workers in the suburbs of Recife. He married a primary school teacher called Elza Maria Oliveira who was Catholic like him. They had five children, two boys and three girls. In 1959 he completed his doctoral thesis in the field for which he was to become famous – that of adult illiteracy. He accepted a professorship in history and philosophy at the University of Recife, which later made him the director of their literacy *outreach programme*. After the death of his first wife he had fallen in love with and married another educator and she remained both his partner and a powerful influence throughout her life. Through talking to her he became more and more interested in how people learn and how they should be taught.

He became involved with the state-run trades unions and through this was appointed director of the Department of Education and Culture in the Social Service for Industry (or SESI) in 1954.

The intersection between the work of Paulo Freire and the world of early childhood development

It is here that we find the first overlap between the work for which he is famous – adult literacy – and the learning and development of young children. His time with SESI involved him going into their schools and kindergartens to consider how the earliest years of education operated and it was here that he started to think about and discuss the education of young children. One of the things he tried to do was to involve the students themselves and their parents and family members together talking about educational and social issues. He believed that issues affecting the lives of people like malnutrition or child labour could only be dealt with and possibly resolved with the participation of parents and community members. This is an example of his *sociocultural approach*. The famous Italian educationalist *Loris Malaguzzi* qualified as a teacher at the end of the Second World War and, determined to improve life chances for the children of the poor, he soon recognised the importance of inviting parents to participate in the design of educational policies. He realised that it was essential to take account of where the children lived, in what conditions and with access to what facilities. He was face to face with the issues of poverty, illiteracy, alienation and apathy. Malaguzzi was successful in gaining the support of the local authority. By contrast SESI did not want the involvement of students and their families in their facilities. Nor were they prepared to listen to Freire's words on the importance of dialogue, respect, democratisation, participation and self-government. He resigned, probably within moments of being dismissed.

Back in Recife he started to look at the issue of adult illiteracy among the poor people of that city and as he did so he became more and more politicised. Between 1947 and 1959, his involvement with adult literacy intensified. He became increasingly dissatisfied with the traditional methods for dealing with illiteracy that seemed regularly to operate on the basis of an authoritarian relationship between teacher and pupil (Elias 1994: 3). In effect the die was cast. The work he began when analysing how illiterate adults were taught was the start of his long journey into the world of pedagogy – a journey we will follow in the chapters to come. But now we move on to the story of his life as his time in Brazil came to an ugly end.

Going into exile

On 1 April 1963 there was a military coup in Brazil to remove the leftist President Goulart. He had an affinity for Marxist ideals and was concerned about the plight of the enormous number of destitute people in the countryside and some of the cities. He had started to initiate some social reforms focusing specifically on the poorest people in northeast Brazil. Soon after the coup Freire was arrested and held without charge for seventy-five days. On his release he was offered exile and fearing a life under the extreme right-wing government of the day he made the decision to go. Here is what he said:

> No one goes anywhere alone, least of all into exile – even those who arrive physically alone, unaccompanied by family, spouse, children, parent or siblings. No one leaves his or her world without having been transfixed by its roots, or with a vacuum for a soul. We carry with us the memory of many fabrics, a self soaked in our history, our culture; a memory, sometimes scattered, sometimes sharp and clear, of the streets of our childhood, of our adolescence; the reminiscence of something distant that suddenly stands out before us, in us, a shy gesture, an open hand, a smile lost in a time of misunderstanding, a sentence, a simple sentence possibly now forgotten by the one who said it. (Freire 2009: 23)

This gives you a taste of his writing. It is almost poetic and creates a vivid sense of what he felt he had lost. You will appreciate that he wrote in Portuguese so we always – or nearly always – read him in translation. But perhaps this will give you the flavour of his style and invite you to read some of his books, many of which are wonderful.

He went first to the embassy in La Paz in Bolivia, waiting there for more than a month for the safe-conduct pass without which he could not leave. That first night, before he was overcome with altitude sickness, he longed for home and began to think about how this terrible longing could turn into him remembering, falsely, all that was good and nothing of what he had been fighting for in Brazil. He arrived in Chile in November of 1964, first in Arica and then on to Santiago and so great was his relief at being able to breathe normally and walk with ease after the difficulties he had endured at high altitude that he wrote that he felt human again. In his own words 'Long live oxygen!' (2009: 26).

A few days after arriving in Chile he began working as consultant for an economist and it was only in mid January of 1965 that he was reunited with his wife and children. Faced with the enormous task of all of them adapting to a new country and culture he nonetheless wrote that Chile received them 'in such a way that the foreignness was turning into comradeship, friendship, siblingship. Homesick as we were for Brazil, we had a sudden special place in our hearts for Chile, which taught us Latin America in a way we had never imagined it' (Freire 2009: 26). Chile, at that time, was a place of hope and optimism. According to Freire, the new Christian Democratic government was a government of neither extreme right nor left. Everyone appeared to have great faith in the armed forces. But their optimism and belief in the army was severely challenged as all who followed the history of the region know. Freire stayed in Santiago until 1969 and during that time he became a consultant to UNESCO. That was the beginning of a long and powerful link in his life.

A digression into the story of the Popular Unity (UP) government

Salvador Allende and the Popular Unity government came to power at the end of 1970. They were a coalition of forces on the left, seeking to put in place what they called an "anti-imperialist" programme of building socialism within a democratic and constitutional framework. Their aims were laudable and had, at their centre, a deep concern for the poor and dispossessed. At the time Chile was in the midst of an economic crisis and it soon became clear that members of the opposition (possibly with the support of the USA) began deliberately to exacerbate these difficult conditions. Wealth was withdrawn from the country, private investment ceased, national production fell and unemployment rose. The new government had to delay their initial aims in order to place economic recovery as its primary immediate goal.

Allende initially raised wages and froze prices, adopting a populist approach to the economic problem which had the incidental political objective of both consolidating and widening support for the government. The result was a substantial increase in consumer spending which, in turn, caused a notable redistribution of income downward. The minimum level of taxable income was raised, a measure which benefited 35 per cent of the people who had paid taxes on their earnings in 1969. The armed forces actually received the full increase in pay that had been promised them by the previous government of Eduardo Frei. Over 330,000 small proprietors were relieved of capital taxes. In joint ventures with private firms, the government increased public works, further reducing unemployment. Between 1970 and 1972, the incomes of 300,000 retired pensioners were raised. Insurance was extended to cover 360,000 small-shop owners and manufacturers, market vendors, artisans, transport workers and other small owners – the very social groups, the "petty bourgeoisie," which had been most vocal in their opposition to the Allende government (http://ada.evergreen.edu/~arunc/texts/chile/torre/UPgov.html).

By the time of their first anniversary in power the state had come to control 90 per cent of what had previously been private banking. More than 70 strategic or monopolistic enterprises had been nationalised, or subjected to state intervention, including the copper, coal, iron, nitrates and steel industries. Under the agrarian reform, 2.4 million hectares had been taken over and given to landless farmers to make the land more productive. The indigenous people of Chile had benefited from the founding of the Indian Development Corporation and the Mapuche Vocational Institute. Free milk to was given to children and unemployment had fallen from 8.4 per cent to 4.8 per cent.

But then the economy began to struggle and the Americans, having lost their economic foothold in Chile, sent in CIA operatives and initiated a system of domestic destabilisation. By the middle of that year, the political climate had darkened and this government of the people fell.

Here is an extract from the piece in *The Guardian* on Friday 14 September 1973 written by Richard Gott.

> According to witnesses inside the Moneda, Chile's presidential palace, the president, Salvador Allende, shot himself on Tuesday afternoon after personally directing the defence of his palace.
>
> With him died Augusto 'el Perro' Olivares, one of Latin America's most well-known and best-liked journalists, and perhaps the president's closest friend and collaborator.
>
> The two men killed themselves after an apparently spirited, if useless, defence of the Moneda against vastly unequal odds.
>
> An account of President Allende's last hours was given to the Santiago correspondent of the Spanish news agency, EFE, by someone who was inside the palace on Tuesday morning.
>
> At 7am, the president was awoken and told that two units of the navy had rebelled at Valparaiso, controlling two of the country's three cruisers. Half an hour later, he arrived at the Moneda, having driven the five miles from his residence, protected by a powerful cohort of armed police.
>
> He promptly broadcast over leftwing radio stations, urging the workers to remain in their factories and at their desks. It seems that he planned to wait for the armed forces 'faithful to their tradition' to come to the rescue of the 'legitimately constituted' government, and to crush the naval rebellion.

He announced repeatedly that he would not resign as president of the republic.

At 8.20, Allende received a message from an Air Force general letting him know that an aeroplane was ready (to) escort him from the country.

He replied bluntly: 'A Chilean president does not take an aeroplane to escape. You should know how to perform your military duty'.

At 10.30, the military junta broadcast their ultimatum, demanding the president's resignation before 11am. Allende told his colleagues that he would only leave the palace dead.

Ignominy

On the radio, he spoke of his intention 'to resist by all means, at the cost of my life: to leave to the ignominy of history the lesson of those who have force but not reason'.

The Chilean national motto is 'Por la razon o la fuerza' – by reason or by force.

After 11.00, it became clear that not a single unit of the armed forces in Santiago had remained loyal to the president.

The civilian staff left the Moneda, leaving the president behind, dressed in a helmet and armed with a machine gun, personally directing the defence of his presidential palace, and in command of 200 loyal policemen.

At midday exactly, the aerial bombardment of the palace began, joined by fire from armoured cars surrounding the palace.

At least 20 bombs were dropped. Part of the Moneda caught fire, and firing continued for a considerable time in the surrounding streets.

Although there have been no official figures for the numbers killed, the EFE correspondent estimates that, given the intensity of the firing, there might easily have been more than 500 casualties.

Armed helicopters fired at the roofs and upper stories of the high buildings surrounding the Moneda. By five in the afternoon, the palace was still smouldering and only its shell remained intact. At 6.30, the armed forces announced that President Allende had surrendered.

But by then, he was already dead. With him, apart from Augusto Olivares, were two of his ministers, Anibal Palma and Daniel Vergara.

'These are the last words you are going to hear from me' he said. 'Trust your leaders: continue to trust the people'.

I quote this in full because it was a defining moment in the lives of many people, one of whom was Freire.

Closing the circle

From April 1969 until February 1970 Freire lived in Cambridge, Massachusetts, where he taught a course on his own ideas as a guest lecturer at Harvard University. After that he moved on to Geneva to act as a specialist consultant to the department of education of the World Council of Churches. In this role he travelled widely throughout parts of Africa, Asia, Australia and America. He spent much of his time working in countries which had overthrown colonialism and become independent in managing their educational systems to ensure that the citizens of these countries could see themselves as full and equal, participating and educated contributors. In his words he insisted that the only way in which people could be liberated was to free themselves from oppression. In 1979 there was a political amnesty in Brazil and Freire received his first Brazilian passport and returned to the country of his birth for a month, in the first instance, and finally to live out his life. His first wife had died and he married again in 1988 to Ana Maria Araujo, whose own words you will encounter in this book.

The influences on him and his thinking

You should by now have a picture of this man and his passions and it will be clear to you that the influences in his life came from many sources. This is true for all of us. Most significant was his life experience. Perhaps the most powerful was growing up amidst poor people and witnessing not only their daily struggle to survive but also the very limited and narrow opportunities offered them through education which was not geared to the life needs and possibilities of the poor and dispossessed. When he began to work with illiterate adults he had to consider both what it was in the teaching they were offered which held them back and what there was in society that kept them passive and silent. He worked too as a lawyer, always in poor communities and always in a political and ethical framework.

He was a thinker and a reader and his life experience led him in the direction of studying and reading about what most interested him. He considered marginalisation and alienation of individuals and groups; the passivity of some learners; the gap between the haves and the have-nots; the ways in which privileged and not privileged people had access to education, culture, money, jobs and power. So you will not be surprised to find these names in the list of writers he read: Karl Marx, Lenin, Castro, Mao Tse Tung, Gramsci, Che Guevara and Frederick Engels. He also read the works of Simone de Beauvoir, Sartre, Marcuse, Lukacs, Hegel, Lucien Goldman and Petrovic.

His theoretical/political framework thus included his life experience and his wide and critical reading. As he worked with different groups of people in different situations and across many countries he was able to contextualise his thoughts, try out his developing ideas and take note of what happened. So he was, on a small scale, also a researcher. He was influenced by both of his wives, his friends and his colleagues. In 1989 he became Minister of Education in Brazil, moving out of the rarified world of academia. In this new post he was responsible for developing and overseeing school reform within two-thirds of the country's schools. He was still in that position when he died in May 1997.

He was the first person to win the King Baudouin International Development Prize in 1980 and the UNESCO 1986 Prize for Education for Peace. He was given an honorary doctorate by the University of Nebraska at Omaha in 1996. Sharing this was Augusto Boal (who you will encounter in this book) during their residency at the Second *Pedagogy and Theatre of the Oppressed Conference* in Omaha.

Looking back, looking ahead

In this first chapter we have looked, briefly, at the life of Paulo Freire from his birth in Brazil through exile abroad and return to Brazil where he eventually died. It was a life dominated by his response to the inequalities he encountered and analysed wherever he went. He saw that the poor people were poorly taught. The result was that they remained passive, not having been given the tools to ask and answer questions. He saw how in countries emerging from the domination of colonial rule or the abuse of power, the people were still struggling to find a voice that might enable them to play the roles of full and active citizenship. He wrote about all that he saw and thought and his books are as relevant today as they were when they were first written.

In the next chapter we examine the development of his ideas on literacy.

Chapter 2

Literacy and beyond

In this chapter we begin to think about some of the most significant aspects of the work of Paulo Freire. He is one of the great figures in education and his work included setting up major literacy programmes in Brazil, Chile, São Tomé and Principe and Guinea-Bissau, amongst other countries. His books have been translated into many languages. He is widely cited in academic books and journals, features in many university courses and has institutions, roads and city squares named after him. He is best known for his work on adult literacy and his critique of existing methods of teaching. Literacy was a key theme for him and it is with this that the book starts. In this chapter we will look at his approach to adult literacy.

Literacy and liberation

Remember, always, that Freire had his roots in both privilege and poverty. He experienced loss and hunger, moved home several times, yet managed to go to good schools and on to university. The death of his father was a tragic loss. He was forced into exile. So he saw the best and the worst of his home country. This almost certainly contributed to his awareness of the impact of poverty, homelessness, ill health and illiteracy on the lives of the majority. This is important because it explains the deeply political nature of all of his work.

For Freire learning to read was seen as a potentially significant feature of the process of liberation from conditions of oppression. For him reading, writing and politics were inextricably linked. According to him not everyone who might claim to be reading is reading. Mechanically repeating words without attempting to understand them and put them in a social, cultural, political context is merely what we might call 'barking at print'. Freire said that such 'readers' may be demonstrating reading behaviours but what they are doing can only be called real reading when it is done critically. It follows that the text – what is read – matters and part of the task of being a critical reader is to understand and analyse what is being read.

Freire abhored the practice of many teachers insisting that students read huge numbers of books, fearing that this devouring of texts does little to help the readers make the links or connections between what is being read and the reader's interests and experience.

Here is what he says about teaching adults to read:

> I always saw teaching adults to read and write as a political act, an act of knowledge and therefore a creative act. I would find it impossible to be engaged in work of mechanically memorising vowel sounds, as in the exercise 'ba-be-bi-bo-bu, la-le-li-lo-lu'. Nor could I reduce learning to read and write merely to learning words, syllables or letters, a process of teaching in which the teacher *fills* the supposedly *empty* heads of learners with his or her own words. On the contrary, the student is the subject of the process of learning to read and write as an act of knowing and of creating. The fact that he or she needs the teacher's help, as in any pedagogical situation, does not mean that the teacher's help nullifies the student's creativity and responsibility for constructing his or her own written language and for reading this language. (Freire and Macedo 1987: 35)

This is a very significant passage and is worth reading again. Perhaps keeping these questions in mind will help make the meaning clear.

• What makes teaching someone to read a political act?
• What does the meaningless memorising of lists of vowel sounds make you think of in terms of your own experience of becoming a reader?
• Why do you think the words 'fills' and 'empty' are italicised?

A student, responding to these questions said this:

> When you are teaching someone to read you are helping them to enter into the minds and ideas and lives of others. This has got to be empowering, particularly for adults who have been denied such access. Memorising vowel sounds made me think of all the meaningless activities many teachers use when teaching children phonics. I feel that starting with the smallest unit of language – the letter – takes away any possibility of making meaning. And reading is all about meaning. I hated the idea of the learners having nothing in their heads until some teacher fills the gap. (With thanks to A.M. 2003)

Reading the world: reading the word

For Freire, *reading the world* – by which he meant making sense of the world and everything in it – must come before reading the word. Reading the word implies constantly and continually reading and rereading the world. In everyday language he was saying the learners must first learn about their world and then learn to read words. Each reading of words, once the learner becomes relatively fluent, changes what the reader thinks and feels and changes her understanding of the world. An understanding of the world is enhanced by reading. So it is a never-ending cycle.

Freire's writing about reading is distinctly not sentimental. He rarely, if ever, focuses on the wonders of literature and for him reading becomes joyous only when the act of reading becomes active, dialogical and critical. A book is only beautiful when the reader engages critically with it.

Here we encounter for the first time one of the key words in his writing. This is the word *conscientization* which is almost synonymous with critical consciousness and/or with consciousness raising. The aim of enabling illiterate adults to read the world is to help them to become critically aware of why they are in the positions in which they exist – poor, perhaps jobless, perhaps with large families, possibly without much hope – and to consider what it is that keeps them there.

Freire's goal was 'to make it possible for illiterates to learn quickly how to write and to read, and simultaneously learn also the reasons why the society works in this way or that way' (Horton, Freire and Bell 1991: 84). Elsewhere Freire examined issues relating to becoming critically conscious and these included attitudes to self, to texts and to ways of being taught.

Here is a wonderful and true story about the power of literacy in altering the lives of people. *The Pajaro Valley experience* was written by Alma Flor Ada in memory of Freire's first wife, the teacher Elza Freire. The chapter describes a project in the Pajaro Valley where researchers worked with Spanish-speaking parents to develop children's reading and writing skills and did this by using children's literature.

> The story tells us that when the father returned home upset, his daughter asked him what was the matter. Upon finding out that he was tired, she continues: "The old man received a big surprise. His little daughter told him. 'Look, Father I have a cure for your tiredness . . . I will tell you a very pretty story that Mother read me from a book' . . . and the story was so amusing that the father forgot how tired he was and he laughed and hugged his little daughter and gave her a kiss".
>
> Araceli, the 5-year-old girl who dictated this story to her older sister Pati, had discovered not only that books can be entertaining but that they offer the possibility of influencing our immediate reality. (Ada 1988: 223–4)

If you read the chapter you will find many of the features of what Freire might have called *liberatory education* in place. The Pajaro Valley School project was exploring the power of literacy as a consciousness-raising tool and also used dialogue and the asking of questions to generate a real exploration of the many issues affecting the lives of the children, their parents and their communities. Teachers and parents, teachers and children, children and parents began to take on the roles of both teacher and learner. The impact of the project and the pedagogy is summed up by one mother who said 'since we began talking every night about the books they are reading, and since they began writing themselves, our two children have become closer, and we feel closer to them' (op. cit.: 234).

Becoming and remaining critically literate in a Freirean sense implies the development of a particular orientation towards the world. Critical reading involves a constant interplay between text and context – hence reading the word, reading the world.

How and why some students become alienated

In *Pedagogy of the Oppressed* Freire said that in order for anyone to be able to claim to be fully human they had to be active social actors who wanted and were able to participate as equal partners in social and political life. Human beings create culture and, according to Freire, have the right to *name the world*. He said:

> Human existence cannot be silent, nor can it be nourished by false words, but only by true words, with which men and women transform the world. To exist, humanly, is to *name* the world, to change it. Once named, the world in its turn reappears to the namers as a problem and requires of them a new *naming*. Human beings are not built in silence, but in word, in work, in action-reflection. (Freire 1996: 69)

This is quite difficult to understand but basically what he is saying is that all human beings have the capacity to look critically at the world. This means that nothing is predetermined: people acting collaboratively and collectively have the capacity to change the world. You will appreciate that when individuals or groups are denied access to thinking about and challenging their world, they become alienated from it and, as we have seen, may become enveloped in a culture of silence. This means that they accept their world as it is, with all its injustice and succumb to a sense of fatalism. It is as if they sit down and sigh and say 'This is just how life is'.

Karl Marx developed a theory of *alienation* and Freire easily identified a major source of oppression within the classed nature of society and the *material conditions* of people's lives. The rich live well, are able to educate their children well, have access to all the benefits of living in privilege; the poor live in bad conditions, with little access to health care or education or well-paid jobs. The rich oppress the poor, alienating them as they do so. At first Freire thought of the oppressed as being the peasants of Brazil but he later recognised that oppression is a global phenomenon. One might argue that the Third World exists within the urban ghettos of cities like London or Paris or New York or Beijing. In his later life Freire became extremely critical of the impact of globalisation and *neoliberal* governance on the poorest members of society. He wrote:

> Exposing the contradictions and diseased reasoning in the so-called 'triumph of capitalism over socialism', he asks: 'what excellence is this [economic system] that manages to coexist with more than a billion inhabitants of the developing world that live in poverty'. (Freire 1994: 90)

Freire's theory of *objectification* (making people merely objects) is not limited to economic factors but encompasses social and cultural forces of domination, such as patriarchy and racism that operate through the state, schools, families, the media and other agencies.

It follows that the challenge is for oppressed people to liberate themselves from the conditions which subjugate them. But, as we have already seen, this becomes less and less possible as people are repeatedly told that this is just how things are and denied the right to question. As a result many become alienated from society and, as part of that, from education. Since it is education which contributes to them accepting their status, they withdraw from it, becoming less and less able to access it and its potential benefits.

We know that in our society it is often young people who become alienated, particularly at times of financial crisis when jobs and money become scarce. It is as though the identity of 'youth' is a commodity which can be acquired through looking and behaving like the figures chosen to represent young people on the media. Young people wear designer clothes, sport the latest mobile phones and use the most up-to date technology. 'This is how young people should be' say the images, but they can rarely attain this because of having no money or status. McInerney refers to this as the 'society of the spectacle' (Frymer 2005: 13, cited in McInerney 2009: 26). Young people with no jobs, no future, spend their time gazing at and aspiring to impossible and useless goals.

On top of this some oppressive schooling arrangements contribute to alienation. This means that schools might become complicit in the objectification of young people when learning is so often disconnected from their lives and aspirations. Students may have little or no say in the choice of curriculum topics or how they might investigate them; they have few opportunities to talk about the life issues that concern them because the timetable requires them to meet particular targets, not related to these interests. What happens is that those teachers who do try and engage them in a critical reading of their own choice often fail because there are so few opportunities for either the teachers or the students to work collectively with their peers to change things.

In relation to this McInerney talks about a project in Australia where four secondary schools allowed their pupils to participate in a research project, part of which involved asking the students what it was that led to them being reluctant to participate in civil society. In other words what was it that kept them alienated? Here are some of their responses:

They said that teachers had difficulties in raising the expectations of students about the relevance of education; in getting large numbers of students involved in classes and learning; in confronting with students issues to do with violence and antisocial behaviour in classrooms and in getting them to talk about their often fractured lives. It will not surprise you to learn that often negative comments about the young people and their families and communities were made, situating the responsibility for their alienation within the students rather than within the system or the society. For example some of the teachers made comments like:

> 'we don't have a lot of academic kids in our school'; 'many of our parents don't value education'; 'staff often tell me that our kids are not motivated'. At the extreme edge of this thinking, a teacher reasoned 'as a general rule 10% [of our students] are bums and 30% are lazy'. Students also internalized and participated in their own oppression. 'I'm too dumb to go to university' claimed a senior secondary student. (McInerney 2009: 29)

The teachers did not talk about alienation but rather mentioned some of the attitudes common in society – such as racist, sexist and homophobic attitudes and language – which impacted on the self-image of students. All the schools in the project had respectful written policies but bullying in the school yard or playground persisted despite this. Government proposals offered as possible solutions, like raising the school leaving age, merely forced already reluctant young people to stay in school for an additional year.

The intersection between the work of Paulo Freire and the world of early childhood development

You will almost certainly know of some young children who are alienated from the mainstream and seem to struggle from their earliest days of being in a nursery or primary school or children's centre. They may come from marginalised groups – immigrants, speakers of languages other than English, poor, having suffered some life traumas, have learning or other difficulties. As we have seen, people are oppressed in many ways and for many different reasons. It is true that most of those who work with the youngest children are sensitive to their individual needs and, because the ratios of adults to children are better than they are when the children are older, manage to respond to their individual needs and interests. But here are a few examples where you might have to think hard about what it is that is causing a child difficulties. The question to ask is 'Is the fault (if there is one) situated within the learner (child, family, community) or within the system (school, setting, available resources, training of the adults)'. There is always the possibility of the answer to this question being 'both'.

Gurmit's story:

I was seven years old when we arrive in the United Kingdom. My father came here two years before us. I could not speak or understand a word of English. I remember going to the infant school and sitting there looking around and getting frustrated. Other children used to laugh at me and bully me in the playground. I didn't know how to complain and started to respond by kicking and pushing them. After a couple of months I started to understand the playground language but still found it very hard to cope with the class-work. At the end of junior school I still could not read or spell even basic words . . . Mum and Dad didn't know anything, they worked long hours and I didn't want to worry them. (Statham 2008: ix)

Written by a newly appointed advisory teacher using "A Language in Common" (2000):

S is a 6-year-old Bangladeshi girl in this school who arrived three months previously to live with her father at her uncle and aunt's house. I had already set up a home school contact book and tried to involved the aunt (main carer who speaks little English) and her daughter, S's cousin, to help. I had explained the importance of involving S's cousin in home school liaison. (Statham 2008: 52)

Tony, the class clown:

Tony is four years and three months old and he attends a nursery class for a second year. He is a clever, intelligent and exceptionally creative boy. He is also the 'clown' of the class. Against all the teacher's efforts, Tony's behaviour remains a challenge for her, the other staff and the children in the nursery. Tony always finishes his work quickly, without completing it. When the nursery teacher, Mrs Rose, encourages him to look at his work again and make some effort, he replies that he has finished and his work is good. (Papatheodorou 2005: 5)

It is easy to see just how each of these young children has been oppressed in some way through being different from the mainstream. Gurmit's inability to communicate in his new school and country led to him lying to his parents and withdrawing from school. It seems the school did little to support him or take notice of how he was behaving. S, by comparison, is entering a school in a forward-looking local authority, where the advisory teacher is clearly putting in place some structures within the family and the school in order to support this young child's learning and development. I wonder how you responded to the example of Tony. My analysis is that this very bright child is being asked to engage with formal learning, remote from his own interests, in a formal learning situation, not suited to such a young child. Do come back to this question when you have read more about the dangers of what Freire called *banking education*.

Looking back, looking ahead

This chapter has been concerned with looking at the links between learning, power, oppression and alienation. In following Freire's political analysis of the importance of reading in order to participate in the everyday world we have spent some time thinking about oppression and its consequences and started to think about reading the world and then reading the word. In the next chapter we continue to look at literacy and start by defining illiteracy.

Chapter 3

Dialogue, illiteracy and more

This chapter starts by explaining some of the important ideas underpinning Freire's work. Like all of us he arrived at a particular view of the world based on his own experience and what he learned from that. By now you know something about his life in Brazil, into exile and eventually becoming a world-renowned expert on and advocate for a particular way of teaching – teaching for equity, liberation and civil participation. Because he had lived in a divided society where the gap between the rich and the poor was enormous, he began to analyse what it was that caused the tremendous social and economic inequalities. He thought and wrote about just what it means to be human; the impact illiteracy has on individuals and groups; the influence of the work of Gramsci on his thinking and more on what he meant by reading the word and reading the world. You will encounter more terms which might be unfamiliar to you, but each is explained in everyday language and definitions of each of these terms can be found in the glossary at the end of the book.

What does it mean to be human?

You might like to answer the question yourself. What do you think it means to be human? Some people respond by saying that having emotions is what makes us human. Others say the need to have other people in our lives makes us human. Some say that possessing language is what makes us human. Some arrive at a more physiological definition – stand upright, have opposing thumbs and forefingers and binocular vision, for example. For Freire the essence of being human is to be in dialogue or encounters with others, *mediated* by the world, in order to name the world and transform it. This is a lot to take in so we will go step by step.

- The word *ontological* means the essence of being human.
- Freire believed that all human beings have what he called an *ontological vocation* to become more human.

- What he meant by this is that human beings are driven to be more fully human, in the sense of being more part of the groups of other humans and entitled to equal rights and respect.

Freire insisted that the process of becoming more human is under-pinned by values of mutual respect, humility, trust, faith, love, hope and critical thinking. If we move away from the complex language all we are saying is that *we are social beings who live in groups, where we communicate with one another, make and use tools which define our culture, make and share meanings.* We expect to be full contributing and respected members of our society. But we also know, if we think about it, that there are others in our community who may be out of work, poor, immigrant or illiterate who are often accorded little respect and few if any tools to enable them to participate fully in the life, culture, development and systems of their country.

Freire believed that what makes us distinct as a species involves several features which are closely tied to one another.

o The first is *consciousness* or an awareness that we are separate from but involved in the world. We not only live in the world but can act on it and expect it to react to what we do. For Freire, the word *world* describes everything that takes place wherever any human being is. Acting on the world means taking action alone or with others to try and change something in or about the world. For example, a worker who loses her job does not necessarily lie down and accept it. She may join with other people in the same position, realising that acting together is more likely to change a position than working alone. What the worker is doing is *consciously seeking to change the world by her actions.* It is our consciousness of the world and of the possibilities of change (however unlikely) which make this happen.

o The second is that human beings are constantly questioning and changing the world. Freire's phrase for this is that humans are *beings of praxis* (a term he borrowed from Marxist philosophy). Here is what Freire wrote as a definition of beings of praxis.

> As beings of the praxis (humans) differ from animals, which are beings of pure activity. Animals do not consider the world. They are immersed in it. In contrast humans emerge from the world, objectify it and in so doing understand and transform it with their labour. . . . (Human) activity consists of action and reflection. It is praxis; it is transformation of the world. And as praxis it requires theory to illuminate it. (Human) activity is theory and practice. (Freire 1972: 96)

Praxis is both action and reflection which means doing something consciously.

o   The third feature is that humans are not complete or perfect but, in
    Freire's terms, are humanised in *dialogue*. Dialogue is a key theme
    and a rather difficult one to explain. We have touched on it and
    will return to it again and again. It has the everyday meaning of an
    exchange between people and relates to the fact that humans are
    born into and live in communities made of up other humans with
    whom they constantly interact. You will see that Freire's position is
    essentially a sociocultural one. Interactions depend largely on lan-
    guage. It is through language that we are able to name the world
    which, according to Freire, is how voiceless people can find a voice.
    Here we have to deal with his deep concern with what he called
    conscientization (a word he borrowed from Frantz Fanon) which
    means developing consciousness, where consciousness is under-
    stood to have the power to transform reality (Taylor 1993: 52).
    Here is an example to illustrate this:

> In Mali an NGO working with illiterate rural people first tried to
> teach the students literacy in a traditional formal way of teach-
> ing them to make the sounds of letters, blend them together and
> say aloud the words. They were aiming at making these people
> functionally literate. The results showed that learning to decode
> like this made no difference to the ways in which the learn-
> ers saw themselves or how they were able to effect changes. It
> was only when the educators changed their approach to helping
> the students learn to read so that they might understand and
> question – and in this way conscientized them – that the stu-
> dents became aware of their own needs and potential powers.

Here is how Freire himself explained his ideas on *conscientization*:

> As we attempt to analyse dialogue as a human phenomenon,
> we discover something which is the essence of dialogue itself:
> *the word*. But the word is more than just an instrument which
> makes dialogue possible; accordingly, we must seek its con-
> stitutive elements. Within the word we find two dimensions,
> reflection and action, in such radical interaction that if one is
> sacrificed – even in part – the other immediately suffers. There
> is no true word that is not at the same time a praxis. Thus, to
> speak a true word is to transform the world.
>   An unauthentic word, one which is unable to transform real-
> ity, results when dichotomy is imposed upon its constitutive
> elements. When a word is deprived of its dimension of action,
> reflection automatically suffers as well; and the word is changed
> into idle chatter, into *verbalism*, into an alienated and alienating
> 'blah'. It becomes an empty word, one which cannot denounce

the world, for denunciation is impossible without a commitment to transform, and there is no transformation without action.

On the other hand, if action is emphasized exclusively, to the detriment of reflection, the word is converted into *activism*. The latter – action for action's sake – negates the true praxis and makes dialogue impossible. Either dichotomy, by creating unauthentic forms of existence, creates also unauthentic forms of thought, which reinforce the original dichotomy.

Human existence cannot be silent, nor can it be nourished by false words, but only by true words, with which men and women transform the world. To exist, humanly, is to *name* the world, to change it. Once named, the world in its turn reappears to the namers as a problem and requires of them a new *naming*. Human beings are not built in silence, but in word, in work, in action-reflection. (Freire 1993: 68–9)

This is difficult to understand but if you read it through slowly you will get the gist and be able to make sense of it. In summary what he is saying is that to be human we have to reflect critically on what we see or experience, speak out about it and act on it in order to effect change. And this all takes place in a social and political context.

o   The fourth feature relates to how humans can learn from one another. During his life in Brazil and later in exile he spent time working with poor and illiterate adults in *informal or popular educational programmes* where he observed that *dialogic* relationships between teachers and learners often prevailed. In a dialogic relationship there is no one in charge, but both are equal partners. This allows for the students or learners to follow issues that interest or concern them, which in turn leads to the raising or posing of questions. In dialogue the asking of questions is at least as important and often more important than answering them. So, unlike traditional formal learning situations, informal education is often based on conversation rather than curriculum; respect is shown to everyone; people work together and both show and are shown respect. Dialogue is about more than deepening understanding: essentially it involves making a difference in the world. Dialogue in itself is a co-operative activity involving respect. Freire saw the process itself as enhancing community, building *social capital* and leading those involved to act in ways that make for justice and empowerment. The term *social capital* was first used by Bourdieu and for our purposes it means the links, shared values and understandings that enable individuals and groups to trust each other and so work together. You can see that social capital is something desirable, enabling people to move ahead in life. It is less accessible to those who are poor and illiterate.

The intersection between the work of Paulo Freire and the world of early childhood development

The fifth point about being human is one that will have much relevance for all those involved or interested in the learning of young children. We know that young children will learn best if they can make *human sense* of any learning situation. By making human sense we mean that they can see the point or purpose of any activity and, crucially, are able to draw on their own everyday experience. Freire insisted on situating educational activity in the *lived experience* of participants which means that when he thought about how to teach illiterate adults to read and write he recognised that they needed to be able to read and write about their own concerns which came, directly, from their lived experience. His concern was to look for words that have the possibility of generating new ways of naming and acting in the world.

The scandal of illiteracy

In 2013 there are said to be 774 million people worldwide who can't read and 66 per cent of them are female. In the United States 14 per cent of the population cannot read: an astounding 32 million illiterate people in one of the richest countries in the world.

In the 2011 worldwide census 26 per cent of the population was illiterate. Almost all of these illiterate adults were to be found in only ten countries – India, China, Pakistan, Bangladesh, Nigeria, Ethiopia, Egypt, Brazil, Indonesia and the Democratic Republic of the Congo. All of these regions, except Brazil, are in South and West Asia or Sub-Saharan Africa. Do you regard this as inevitable or as a scandal?

Here are some vignettes to describe the effects of illiteracy. They are drawn from a range of sources.

- Kunte comes from West Africa. He said 'Only the most privileged go to school to learn to read and write and these people become really good at expressing themselves. People like me know what we can't do: we can't say things very clearly. We need help to make sense of almost all situations. We almost certainly can't get jobs because every job requires that you can read or write'.
- Sanjit lives in India and he is having life problems because none of the languages he speaks is one of the official languages. He says that in India illiteracy is very common because in a country which has seventeen official languages many poor people are regarded as being illiterate if they are not fluent in the local or relevant official languages.

- Davinder has two children and has been living in the UK for two years. Her spoken English is reasonable but she can't read or write in English. When her youngest child was ill she was embarrassed at not being able to sign the prescription form (she made a cross). She is also embarrassed by not being able to help her daughter with reading her English books sent home from school.
- Fettouma Touati, born in Algeria, wrote her first novel *Desperate Spring* describing the plight of women in poor and largely illiterate societies. Here is what Fatiha's father said to her:

> 'Tell me, daughter, are you working hard at school? That's the main thing, you know. You don't need to know how to cook or clean. You must study and pass your exams. I know people say that a girl should know how to roll couscous, but I don't want to have lost my mind for nothing. We didn't only go to war for the sake of the boys. If one day you marry a man as helpless as I am, your qualifications will more than make up for him. You must put an end to this poverty and you will forget these miserable years that I have inflicted on you'. (Touati 1987: 6)

Despite the continuing prevalence of illiteracy relatively little is written about it as a matter of deep concern. A UNESCO report in 2010 detailed the effects of illiteracy but some of what they say is disturbing since blame seems to be situated on parents or families rather than on society or education. For example the report says that many young children remain illiterate because their parents are illiterate. This may be true but the fact that there is little analysis of why this is the case is concerning (http://unesdoc.unesco. org/images/0019/001905/190571E.pdf).

What is clear is that poverty itself is a crucial factor but not, as the report suggests, an essential factor. We all know of children from poor families who have succeeded educationally and beyond. There may well be higher levels of illiteracy in poor families than in wealthier families, but the question that Freire asked is the crucial one. He did not ask why there were so many illiterate poor people. Rather *he analysed what society was doing to keep poor people illiterate.* This is a subtle but significant difference and here are the things he noticed:

- Many illiterate people had never been involved in education, certainly not formal education. The ways in which they were taught to read were the ways in which small children were taught to read and that involved being given texts that were meaningless to them and paid no attention to their lived experience which meant that they could not draw on this experience. So illiterate adults were taught to merely decode text. Decoding means working out ways to say the words aloud but does not invite the reader to make meaning or share meaning. This guaranteed that they remained silent, voiceless and not able to ask or answer questions.

- Many illiterate people were apathetic and saw no purpose in learning to read since acquiring a set of limited decoding skills did nothing to improve their social or economic status.
- As a result of not using the reading skills acquired these were soon lost.
- Few illiterate people were aware of having any rights or civil duties and believed that the only jobs that they might be entitled to were of a precarious nature and based on low-quality contracts. The longer they remained passive the more they accepted that in their communities and society, being and remaining poor and illiterate was merely their lot in life. They had no social capital.

It is difficult to put yourself in the shoes of someone who is illiterate but this was something that Freire seemed able to do. Read these case studies and then imagine what each of the people cited must have felt.

The intersection between the work of Paulo Freire and the world of early childhood development

The examples to illustrate this are drawn primarily from the world of early childhood.

- Eight-year-old Ali's mother, suffering from HIV/AIDS went into the local hospital to give birth. He was the breadwinner for the family, not able to go to school because he spent all day collecting plastic bottles to be recycled. With his mother in hospital he had to go to the pharmacy to collect his mother's drugs and because he was illiterate had to remember each item by name.

  o Do you think the pharmacist thought this was a staggering thing for the child to have done? Do you think he blamed the mother or the child or the system?

- Shahanara's family arrived in London from Bangladesh. She needed to be registered at the local school but her mother could not speak English. An English-speaking Bangladeshi woman from the local community accompanied her to the school but neither of the women could read or write in any language.

- o   Do you think the headteacher minded having to fill in the forms herself? Do you think she judged the women?

- • Rohil is in the reception class and the school has a policy for the children to take home a book to read with their parents who are then asked to make a comment about the child's reading in a running record booklet.

- o   How do you think Rohil's illiterate parents feel about this? Do you think they feel unvalued and disempowered? And how do you think the school feels about these parents? Are they seen as not caring, not capable, not deserving of respect?

Literacy and illiteracy: Gramsci and Freire

The Italian social theorist Antonio Gramsci said that *literacy* was not only a concept but also a *social practice* that has to be linked to the ways in which knowledge and power have been constructed over time. For him it was a double-edged sword that could be used for the purposes of self or social empowerment as well as for ensuring the repression and domination of others. The fact that you are reading this book implies that you can all read and write. This means that you have access to the thoughts and ideas of others and can share your thoughts and ideas with others. This allows you access to being part of a community of other literate people who all have the possibility of enjoying access to higher education, better jobs and opportunities to both answer and ask questions. The British National Party has members who are literate and willing and able to write and disseminate hateful and untrue things about immigrants and others. You can see what Gramsci meant about literacy being a double-edged sword.

Literacy is, of course, a *social construct* (which means that it has been developed by human beings) but it can also be seen as a *radical construct*. Radical means far-reaching and a construct is an idea or a theory. In short, literacy can become a precondition for both social and cultural emancipation. By and large, those who are literate have access to education, work, success, power and control; those who are not literate are repressed and dominated however subtly by those who are.

Gramsci used the term *hegemony* to describe the predominance of one social class over others. This may imply not only political and economic control, but also the ability of the dominant class to project its own way of seeing the world so that those who are subordinated by it accept it as 'common sense' and 'natural'. We hear a lot of talk in the UK currently about how a group of young men from one particular class, having been educated at one public school and at Oxbridge, are determining what sort of education our country should have. Some people find it surprising that the poor are not protesting more loudly about proposals which have long-term implications for them and their children. Perhaps, like the disempowered in Brazil, they see it as common sense that they are not worthy of anything more. Paulo Freire said it was obvious that the illiterate people he encountered saw it as only natural that they were inferior in all ways to those who were keeping them in this state. Gramsci noted that 'common sense is not something rigid and immobile, but is continually transforming itself' (Gramsci, quoted in Hall 1982: 73). Freire spoke in almost the same terms when he talked of conscientization.

For both Freire and Gramsci language and power are closely interwoven and offer one of the fundamental ways in which human beings can be agents in constructing the world, making sense of it and organising it in ways of making it seem appropriate for some social practices to be available to different groups in society. Do you feel that all doors are open to you? Think about writers and speakers who use only dense academic language which is not immediately accessible to you, or doctors and lawyers and bankers and financiers who keep you at bay by using language unfamiliar to you. The question you need to ask is whether those using this type of language are intentionally acting as gatekeepers, allowing insiders access and keeping the rest of us out. The importance of this will emerge as we get closer to Freire's ideas on pedagogy or teaching.

Learning to read

In *Literacy: Reading the Word and the World* which Freire wrote with Donaldo Macedo, he gives us a beautifully written description of how he came to learn to read. He believed that to read texts he had first to learn to read the world. This all took place in the house in Recife where he lived as a small child. The house was surrounded by trees and he felt he had an intimate relationship with each tree. He climbed them, experiencing the thrill of taking risks and of being high up. He said:

> The texts, the words, the letters of that context were incarnated in a series of things, objects and signs . . . in the songs of the birds – tanager,

flycatcher, thrush – in the dance of the boughs blown by the strong winds announcing storms; in the thunder and lightening; in the rainwaters playing with geography, creating lakes, islands, rivers and streams . . . in the whistle of the wind, the clouds in the sky, the sky's colour, its movement; in the colour of foliage, the shape of leaves, the fragrance of flowers. . . . (Freire and Macedo 1987: 30) (Note: I have put the text into UK English rather than American spelling.)

At the same time that he was busy making sense of his physical, social and emotional worlds his parents introduced him to reading the word and he said that deciphering each word seemed to flow naturally from reading the world rather than being something superimposed on it. He learned to read in the loving intimate setting of his home with words from his lived experience rather than from his parents' wider world. By the time he went to school he could already read and he was fortunate to have there a teacher called Eunice Vascancello who welcomed this reading child into the world of education and continued to help him read the word-world.

Moving on to secondary school he entered the world of critical reading of texts with the help of the Portuguese teacher. What he said of this is that the texts they analysed were entirely relevant to their interests and passions at the time, so this critical interpretation was not a technical exercise but part of an intellectual quest.

You might find this a rather fanciful and sentimental way of describing learning to read. We know that for many children learning to read is an arduous task, not something that happens as easily as it appears to have been for Freire. Indeed learning to read is onerous for many perhaps because of the ways in which it is taught, the status in which it is held and the access to books and other reading materials. We need to remember that illiteracy is not limited to the developing world nor is it declining significantly. It continues to affect millions of people throughout the world. The important point to remember is that for Freire literacy was about much more than letters and words. It was a form of *cultural politics*. The social geographer Peter Jackson defined cultural politics as 'the domain in which meanings are constructed and negotiated, where relations of dominance and subordination are defined and contested' and for Freire, as for Gramsci and others, the concern was with those who were kept out of participation and *othered* or excluded in some ways. So when Freire set about analysing the faults of formal education and looking for alternatives he was operating within a sociohistorical/cultural, philosophical and political framework. He set about analysing what might be going wrong with formal education and what might be put in its place.

Taken from fiction

As I was writing about reading the world I came across a passage in Ann Patchett's novel *Run* (2008) which chimed directly with what I was thinking. This is a complicated story about families, identity and culture. Two little black boys are adopted by a well-to-do white family who love them and give them all possible opportunities. By chance they come across an eleven-year-old girl who appears to be their sister, although things are far more complex than they seem. She comes from a far poorer background than they do. This little girl goes with the older of her two 'brothers' to his place of work. He is an ichthyologist, passionate about his collection of fish. They go on a very snowy day, a day after he has been hurt in an accident and needs her support, physical and other. He is thrilled that she shows real interest in the fish in their glass containers, and when she brings him one of his most prized examples he asks her to read the label. On the label is the name Henry David Thoreau.

The little girl, Kenya, is silenced by this label, recognising that her brother Tip wants her to say something in recognition, but although she can read the word Thoreau, she has no idea who he was, what he did, why his name was on the label. In Patchett's words:

> She waited a long time, rocking the fish back and forth, knowing that it was something important and that Tip expected that she should be able to figure it out, but she couldn't. None of the words meant anything to her. She breathed and blinked. She tackled it again. It was a test, a kind of reading comprehension test, and if she paid attention to every last detail of what was in her hands she would understand it. She broke down the label word by word, she studied the fish again, and when it was clear that she was never going to come up with anything she closed her eyes and gave it her best guess. 'Are these the only nine sunfish left?' (Patchett 2008)

This is so close to the children and young people I have seen silenced because they are being asked about something to which they have no access. They have no access because it is not part of their experience. They have not had the opportunity to read this aspect of the world.

Tip, recognising her struggle but not realising what caused it prompted her with telling her the names Thoreau and Walden. Now Tip knew and I know and perhaps you know too that Henry Thoreau was a nineteenth-century Renaissance man – a philosopher, environmentalist, poet, essayist and abolitionist. *Walden* is his most famous work.

Tip tried to help her and asked if she had ever been to Walden Pond and of course she had not. Her school had not had the resources to make such trips, however close they were to Boston itself. When Tip offered to take her there she thought it was as likely as going on a trip to the Amazon.

We are poor, not stupid!

In order to make some of the ideas in this chapter clear we will examine a case study that comes from South Africa. Anne Harley (2012), in her article whose title I am using as the subheading for this section, examines some of Freire's ideas in the context of post apartheid South Africa. She is interested in examining the role of *social movements* in social change. Social movements are where groups of people band together because they share a common ideology, view of the world or goal. The *Campaign for Nuclear Disarmament* (CND) was one such social movement: the abolitionists were another; the anti-apartheid campaign a third. Gramsci had argued that if the working class united together they could wage a war of position. This implies that social groups might be capable of believing that change was possible. This may be questionable in the modern world where globalisation and the spread of capitalism are so overwhelming. Some theorists suggest that for there to be real change there needs to be some international movement. If Gramsci was right, however, it makes perfect sense that adult education must have a vital role to play in this, particularly with regard to what might be called *radical adult education* – education which seeks to help people challenge the status quo. In effect this has not been the case and in her writing Harley argues that this might be because adult education has not paid sufficient attention to social movements.

In recent years there has been some work in this field with the effect of getting people to think about how the learning of individuals or groups can be about the active role they can play in *knowledge production*. We are very accustomed to thinking about knowledge transmission (what the teacher passes on to the student) but less to thinking about *knowledge production* (what the learner makes of the knowledge that has been transmitted). In the example of Kenya earlier in this chapter, we saw how the little girl received information (knowledge was transmitted to her through being able to decode the words on the fish label) but she could do nothing with the knowledge because she had nothing in her experience to link it to. She could not produce knowledge because she didn't have the experience which allowed her to raise the question. Perhaps if she had been with a group of learners they could jointly have been able to ask questions which would have given them more access to what they had not all experienced.

Back to South Africa, where, during the course of 2008 six *militants* (a term borrowed from Freire to mean a *critical activist*) met together monthly to discuss what they were learning both through their life experience and formally on a university course. There were two groups of militants, one group engaged as social movement actors on farms (*eplasini*) and the other through social movements in the shacks in which they lived (*eminjondolo*). They had all been sent on the university course by two social movements, the *Rural Network* and *Abahlali baseMjondolo* (the people of the shacks). The militants called these sessions *Living Learning* and the notes they kept were eventually put together into a book by Figlan *et al.* (2009).

In this study two groups of poor and oppressed people had the opportunity to attend a two-year part-time university course. You might want to pause at this point and consider what questions you think they might have taken back from their university session to their communities. I would suggest that they must certainly have recognised how relatively privileged they were in being able to attend a university course. So something of this must have affected how they perceived what they were learning in relation to their everyday lives.

Since the end of apartheid the country has seen the rich get richer and the poor poorer, with the gap between them ever widening. There is a very high unemployment rate, little access to water and electricity and a fixed class structure that may have been deracialised but is certainly not declassified. So now it seems it is the poor – the lowest class – who are unemployed, poorly educated and bitter. They may, as the title of this section says, be poor but they are not stupid. The everyday lives of the militants are based in either the shacks or the farms, both of which cultures formed the social movements which arose in response to their ongoing struggles to ameliorate their lives.

It is important to know something about the university course and how it came about. It was, as we have said, part-time, in order to allow potential students to continue to earn some money whilst they study. It was designed to specifically target underprivileged and often older adults involved in some aspect of community improvement or action. Dialogic engagement with the students was an expectation of both students and teachers. Students were expected to ask and answer questions and to raise the issues which preoccupy them. The teachers are trained to listen and respond to as well as to respect the students. Students are allowed access to this university-level course with less than traditional requirements. The aims of the course are to:

- develop skilled practitioners in the field of adult education and community development, particularly in marginalised communities;
- give access to students who might not otherwise be admitted on the basis of their prior educational levels;
- enable access to students having financial difficulties or time or access constraints by running the programme on a part-time once-a-week basis.

Based on the ideas of Freire and Kolb and using the model of students being active constructors of meaning the programme uses *participatory pedagogy, learning* and *critical education*. You will know that this means that the approach will be to address issues that matter in the lives of the students on the basis of dialogue where teachers and students both play roles of teacher and learner. Learners will be explicitly invited to ask rather than merely answer questions.

In the notes the militants made they agreed with Freire that education can never be neutral or innocent, but is always biased and used for *domestication*. They saw it as their duty to take back education to make it work for them. This is a very important aim and it is important that you understand it. For the militants much of education was seen as *mind dispossession* or *mental abuse*. These are very dramatic terms. Here is what they said:

> We see that education is mostly used to control people and keep power for the powerful – but we can disrupt this. This requires us to analyse what kind of education is going on – is it there to make us 'good boys and girls' or is it helping to make us question things and make that part of our struggle to change the world. (Figlan *et al.* 2009: 20)

(Note: You may need to know that calling black adults 'girl' and 'boy' was common and abusive in the apartheid era.)

The militants identified another critical aspect of education which is that education is often equated with knowledge and it follows that those who have education have knowledge: those who don't are without knowledge – or stupid. They felt that universities – the very seats of higher education – were complicit in this. They concluded that there were three types of education, as follows:

> . . . there is 'education' that is imposed to keep the people suppressed and silent so that the status quo is not threatened. On the other side there is a *liberating education* that starts with the people's struggles to be fully human. But is there a special kind of 'education' in the middle – usually called 'capacity building' or 'political education' – that civil society organisations specialise in giving when people who are meant to be suppressed start to struggle against their oppression? This kind of education is done in the name of the poor and oppressed and is aiming to teach the language and rules of how to change your struggle so that it can be 'in order', following the protocols, thinking and expectations of the civil society people who want to claim to represent the people's struggles and interests. (Ibid.: 47)

For both Gramsci and Freire education had to become dialectical with the teacher being also a learner and the learner being also a teacher. Dialectical teaching involves the raising and asking of questions, discussing possible responses and, where possible, putting what is agreed into action.

Looking back, looking ahead

In this chapter we have laid some foundations for moving into more detail about what Freire thought and wrote. We started by stating Freire's ideas about what makes human beings unique as a species and then examined the impact of literacy in terms of lack of power, access, status and voice. This led to a digression into looking at what is meant by literacy and the chapter ends with what Freire said about how he learned to read not only words but also his world. In the next chapter we look at naming, reading and writing the world. We are, in effect, thinking more about language.

Chapter 4

Naming, reading and writing the world

In this chapter we will look in more detail at what Freire said about the importance of naming, reading and writing the world and the word. Most of this will come from the book he wrote jointly with Donaldo Macedo as they shared their experience and thoughts: Macedo's in the United States and Freire's in Guinea-Bissau as well as in Brazil. You may find some of the methods he initially used to teach adults to read rather strange but they are certainly unusual and it was from this basis that he later developed his influential ideas about teaching and learning. We start this chapter with an analysis of how children acquire and construct language.

How humans acquire and construct language

The intersection between the work of Paulo Freire and the world of early childhood development

All human infants acquire language during their earliest years. Language is a communicative process and a way of both making and sharing meaning. Many years ago it was believed that children acquired language primarily through imitation and reinforcement. The child makes a sound; the adult interprets the sound as meaningful and praises the child; the child repeats the sound. Put crudely the model can be explained like this:

The child babbles and within the string of sounds comes something that sounds like 'mama'.

The mother thinks the child has learned to say the word for mother and kisses the child.

The praise – the positive reinforcement – makes the child say the word again, hoping for another kiss (or hug or banana).

The child has learned to say 'mama'.

But can that possibly be the whole story? Read on. If you have children you can probably remember when your first child said her first word. Or perhaps you remember friends with children describing with amazement their children's first words. Clearly using language to communicate is a milestone in development. What is fascinating is that this remarkable intellectual feat, which usually takes place within the first year of life, occurs without anyone giving the child lessons. No one sets out to teach the child to talk. Rather, children begin to communicate with other beings through gesture, eye-pointing, expression, intonation and eventually through talk. In this social world children are surrounded by people who use talk in many, many different situations in order to communicate. The talk children encounter in their homes and communities is talk for real purposes and between people who want to share meaning. There are no tests to fail or trick questions to answer. So the human infant, working hard to understand communication, does so in the supportive company of people who want to communicate with her. We could say that the infant is in a dialogic relationship to others in her community. The infant cannot yet share meaning but her attempts at it are taken seriously and she is spoken to rather than tested.

Noam Chomsky, an American thinker and writer who is still alive, was the first to suggest that language acquisition is genetically determined. He believed that the human infant was born preprogrammed to work out the rules of speech. If you think about it you will realise that speech — in any language — must be rule-governed if people are to be able to understand it, use it, and be understood. The rules relate to the grammar of any language. In English, for example there are rules about the order of words. We can say 'the dog jumped over the fence' but if we say 'the fence jumped over the dog' it makes no sense because a fence cannot jump. If we say 'the jumped fence the over dog' we are uttering a string of exactly the same words but in an order that prevents it from being meaningful. The same rule does not necessarily apply to other languages. In English we have rules about how we use verbs when we talk about the past tense. So we say 'we walked' and 'we talked': the rule being that we usually add 'ed' to the end of the verb. We have rules about how to talk about more than one object. So we talk about shoes and socks and pens and pencils. The rule here is that we usually add the letter 's' to the end of a noun to make that noun plural. You, as a fluent speaker of the language, will know that there are exceptions to the rules. And this is where Chomsky's brilliance emerged. We fluent speakers of the language say 'went' instead of 'goed' and 'flew' instead of 'flied'; we talk of sheep instead of sheeps. Chomsky noticed that young children, having started out by saying things correctly through imitating what they heard adults and fluent speakers say, move on to making mistakes by applying the rules to all situations. The way in which he described this was that the children were overgeneralizing the rules. He used this as evidence that children are brilliant thinkers, working out the patterns they hear to make up the rules and then, logically, applying them to all situations. So if we analyse this in terms of dialogue we find that the children, through their many interactions with fluent speakers of their language, adult and children, are raising questions about how language works. These questions are implied rather than spoken, but the fact that children change their verbal behaviour suggests that they are inventing theories to explain what they are noticing. Chomsky believed that it was these errors that reveal that children must have something that allows them to use the patterns they hear to work out the rules. What he proposed was that the structure of language, by which he meant the rules that bind it together to make it meaningful, depends on what he called a Language Acquisition Device (LAD).

Many theorists accept that all children are potentially competent users of language from birth. When Chomsky used the term *competence* he meant the capacity to access the underlying and subconscious knowledge of the rule system for generating language. He believed that human infants were born with this. The errors or the mistakes children make show us the efforts they are making to find the patterns in the particular language, to work out the rules and apply them.

Here is an example to make this more clear:

> Fifteen-month-old Antonio points to the plastic farm animals he is playing with and says – 'cows, horses, sheep'.

Here you can see that this very young child is imitating the correct form of plurals he has heard the fluent speakers in his world use. He has not yet worked out the pattern that operates in English for making plurals. One might say that he is 'just copying'.

> But at the age of three Antonio points to the plastic sheep and labels them 'sheeps'.

He has moved on from making a grammatically correct response to making a mistake. Chomsky believed that this was because Antonio had always been paying attention to what he heard, as all human infants do. At first when he spoke he copied the models he had heard. He had always heard of sheep and never of sheeps. But with experience he worked out that adults have a pattern for making plurals: they add an 's' at the end of the word. At first Antonio used this pattern or rule to form all plurals: he hasn't yet learned what we know – that there are often exceptions to the rules. The consequence is that he overapplies or overgeneralises the rule to all situations. No amount of correction at this stage will enable him to rectify his errors. It is only when he has discovered that there are rules and exceptions to rules that he will be able to use both forms. In other words, only with experience of listening to experienced others will he self-correct.

Jerome Bruner was an American psychologist who was both influenced by and critical of the work of Chomsky. He saw a gap in Chomsky's theory and that gap was the lack of any reference to other people, which means a lack of reference to interaction, society, culture or context. For Bruner the development of language requires at least two people involved in negotiation. So language is dialogic by its very nature. The purpose of language is communication and it is through communication that meaning is made and shared and fine-tuned. So, building on Chomsky's LAD, Bruner proposed a more sociocultural model which he called the Language Acquisition Support System (LASS). He conceived of this as a kind of adult scaffolding system. What happens is that children learn their language through their interactions with others, who cue the children's responses and share meanings with them in particular contexts and within cultures. So Bruner adds a sociocultural dimension to Chomsky's model.

It is very important to remember that when children first learn language, they both listen and talk as an intrinsic part of sharing their interests with family/household members and of engaging in joint activities, from getting dressed to asking for a drink to having a temper tantrum. They learn language in the context of real life and for real purposes. In the process they learn the forms and patterns of the language of their community and, at the same time, they learn how to make sense of their experience in the same way as those with whom they interact. It is evident that in these everyday conversational exchanges there is no overt teaching about language. Bakhtin (1986) said that language is not encountered or learned as an abstract system of decontextualised rules and definitions. It occurs as dialogue. Sounds and words are constructed and understood in relation to the specific purposes and conditions of the activity in which they occur and in relation to the utterances that both precede and follow them. As he puts it, 'the forms of language and the typical forms of utterances . . . enter our experience and our consciousness together, and in close connection with one another' (1986: 78). So language is dialogic by nature and in expanding on the dialogic nature of language use, Bakhtin drew attention to what he called its essential *responsivity*, and to the closely related concept of *addressivity*. Let's expand this to make the meaning clearer. In any exchange or conversation, the listener is not passive. She listens and responds in some way, perhaps by smiling or nodding or making a verbal response. So for speakers, responsivity works in both directions. Not only are their words directed towards someone and shaped in anticipation of that person's ability to both understand and respond, which is what Bakhtin calls their addressivity, but they are also responses to preceding utterances, expressing the speaker's attitude to them as well as to the topic of the current utterance. Thus, 'any utterance is a link in a very complex organized chain of other utterances' (1986: 104).

The acquisition of language starts before birth as the foetus can already hear sounds in utero, including that of the spoken voice. From birth the human infant begins to make sense of the world, using all means possible. She looks and listens, touches and tastes, smells and acts on the people and objects she encounters. In this social world she hears the languages of her community and interacts with people in many different situations. This is all part of her naming, reading and writing her world. Freire believed the writing of the world involved acting on the world and in small ways changing it. The child who touches her cup with a spoon produces a sound: a tiny change in the world. In effect, all we are saying is that before a child can learn to write or read she must first have come to understand the world and the effect she can have on it. So, for Freire, reading the world is an essential precursor to reading words and writing the world, a precursor to writing words. Is naming the world what comes first?

As you already know Freire believed that *naming* the world was very important. It is the giving of names to objects, events, actions and people. Young children acquiring their first language or languages do so by naming or labelling first of all the objects and the people in their lives. It is totally culture bound. What the infant encounters are the things that make up her world, her culture.

The first utterances of any infant relate to the things and people and events in their own lives. Freire was not interested in how human infants begin to speak but he was very interested in how people use everyday language to unveil the complex and hidden roots of oppression. It is in the naming of the world that communication plays a central role alongside dialogue as the necessary communicative mode for participatory development, which means just what it says – everyone involved can and should be an active participant. By encouraging students to name their worlds, teachers validate their pupils' humanness. This is something to keep in mind as you read more about Freire's ideas and approach.

The development of culture circles

One of the earliest methods of teaching Freire developed was the *culture circle*. This was a group of adult learners, almost always illiterate adults, gathered together with a coordinator rather than a teacher. The style of teaching involved dialogue rather than lectures accompanied by images, pictures and narrative plus some linguistic analysis. In these groups discussions were held on topics of interest to the students. Examples might be the rising cost of staple foods; the effects of flooding on daily life; the failure to get children to school. Over time the culture circles became the site of adult literacy classes.

The first recorded attempt was in Recife with a group of five illiterate adults, two of whom dropped out very early on. The students all came from rural areas and all felt alienated from formal education and totally accepting of their inabilities to read, write or question. Freire and his colleagues wanted to develop a literacy programme which addressed the real issues drawn from the life experiences of the students. They decided that the programme needed to be developed in particular ways to ensure the following:

- that the students in each session would be *active, dialogical, critical and involved*;
- that the content of the programme was *flexible and open to change*;
- that the techniques used would include what Freire called the *breakdown of themes and codification*.

To make sure that everyone involved understood the terms clearly Freire made the distinction between *dialogue* (which involved communication, interaction and empathy between those involved in order to foster a critical attitude) and *anti-dialogue* (which involved handed-down information, no empathy and answering rather than asking questions).

Freire worked with a team of anthropologists, educators and students in Brazil on a complex plan to develop a programme of initial literacy instruction in the language of Portuguese for rural peasants and villagers. The initial phase of the plan consisted of a prolonged period of social research within the communities where the programme was to be implemented. Members of the literacy team spent time in those communities, participating in informal conversations with residents, observing their culture and listening to their life stories. They felt that they needed to know as much as possible about the vocabulary of the communities, looking for recurring words and themes to be included in materials for the literacy programme. Only when the research and the data collection was complete were they ready to present the programme to those in the culture circles.

The plan for implementing the programme in the cultural circles was detailed and complicated. It went something like this:

• In Phase 1 the coordinators set out to *establish the vocabulary of the group*. You will see how this relates to naming and it is not difficult to recognise that the vocabulary of each group would differ since each is dependent on the lived lives of the members of the student group. It is likely that the everyday vocabulary of people living by the sea would relate to activities like fishing and trawling; those working on the land to planting and harvesting; those in urban slums to transport and street culture. In this first phase the coordinators recorded what was said, taking notes of both the common vocabulary and any key words. This collection of the language of a particular group or circle is interesting in that it is very attentive to how closely language is tied not only to the everyday lives, but also the serious concerns of the members of the group. Freire and Macedo offer some moving examples of what was said.

> 'I want to learn to read and write . . . so that I can stop being the shadow of other people'.
> 'The month of January in Angicos is a hard one to live through because January is a tough guy who makes us suffer'.
> 'I am not angry at being poor but at not knowing how to read'.
> (Freire and Macedo 2001: 87)

• In Phase 2 the coordinators identify key words, the words which appear to be most significant for the students and often carry emotional content. These are the words that are most charged with background meaning for the people. Freire called them *generative words* because he believed that they might have power to generate other words for the learners. The generative words come from the original vocabulary collected and they are chosen according to certain linguistic criteria: they must be phonemically rich; vary in phonetic difficulty so that there is some progression from easy to difficult; and vary in pragmatic tone, which relates to how deeply the word is embedded in the lived worlds of those using it. Unless you have studied linguistics, as Freire had, these are technical terms. Like syllables that can be separated from each other and recombined to form other words. Freire said that, in Portuguese only fifteen words are needed to generate all the other words in the language. The most important criterion for the choice of a word is that it must have the capacity to address the social, cultural and political reality of the lives of the learners.

- Phase 3 is where *codifications are created*. Codifications are simply a way of visually representing aspects of the lives of people. It is a way of gathering information in order to build up a picture or image related to real situations and people. Here are some examples:

> In one group, when someone mentioned that they worked with clay changing something natural through their physical work, the codification was a drawing of people making clay pots on a wheel.
> In another group the codification is a drawing of a local man hunting birds and using a rifle rather than a bow and arrow.

The representations are intended to work as a challenge – something like a coded problem-solving exercise with elements that need to be decoded. The term *decodification* is used to describe the process whereby the people in a group begin to identify with aspects of the situation until they feel themselves to almost be in the situation and can reflect critically upon its various aspects, thus gathering understanding. It is like a photographer bringing a picture into focus. The generative words are set into the codifications and graded according to their phonetic difficulty. One generative word might embody a complete situation or refer to only one aspect of the situation.

- Phase 4 is where *agendas are elaborated* as aids for the coordinators with no particular significance for the learners.
- Phase 5 involves the preparation of *cards with the breakdown of the phonemic families* which correspond to the generative words. For many English-speaking readers this is the most confusing bit of the process and I think that this is because English is a less syllabic language than Portuguese. It is important to know that this final phase was in keeping with established syllabary techniques frequently used to teach word-attack skills in phonetically and orthographically regular

languages such as Spanish and Portuguese. (See Gudschinsky 1967.) Recently, however, some Freirean practitioners working in Basic English in the Native Language (BENL) programs in the United States have begun to question the validity of total reliance on the syllabary method and are urging a shift towards more use of 'whole-word' and 'text-focused' methods (Rabideau, 1989).

Let's make this easier to understand by attempting to analyse two words syllabically, one in Portuguese – with thanks to Freire – and one in English.

The word *tijolo* means brick and was one of the generative words which came out in a discussion with construction workers. Initially the members of the culture circle were shown the word actually written on a real brick. Then the word was broken down into its constituent syllables *ti-jo-lo* and the group was presented with each syllable in turn and asked to learn the whole phonemic family. So for the first syllable *ti* the group arrived at *ta, te, ti, to, tu*; for the second *ja, je, ji, jo, ju* and so on. It is easy to work out the pattern – each initial consonant followed by each of the vowels in turn. After much discussion about this the group was given a *Discovery Card* on which they found the full breakdown of the syllables.

ta-te-ti-to-tu
ja-je-ji-jo-ju
la-le-li-lo-lu

Now, for fun, try this for yourselves. Reading horizontally and vertically make up as many words as you can using the syllables. Here are some of mine – *tojolo*, *luta* (which I happen to know means struggle) and *lejeta*. Only one of these is a real word. The groups cited in Freire's work managed to create many real words and in one amazing example there is the person who wrote on the board *o povo vai resouver os poblemas do Brasil votando conciente* which means 'the people will solve the problems of Brazil by informed voting!' (Freire and Macedo 2001: 91). Extraordinary!

Now let's take an English word and this will be more difficult for English is less of a syllabic language than Portuguese. I have chosen the word *carpenter*. This has three syllables which are *car-pen-ter* (and interestingly two of those syllables are words in their own right – *car* and *pen*). Here is our new discovery card:

car-cer-cir-cor-cur
pan-pen-pin-pon-pun
tar-ter-tir-tor-tur

Try as I might I cannot make new words from these syllables.

I wonder how you feel about this as an approach to teaching people to read. For me what is positive is respecting and reflecting the real lives and issues of the learners in the teaching materials and methods. Doing this through finding out about the vocabulary of the learners to find points of contact and common interest in the group is relevant. But the emphasis on breaking the words down into small letter groups flies in the face of how I think we best teach children to read. You might want to consider this approach and think about the current fashion for teaching children to read in this country primarily through using phonics. There are strong parallels in the sense of both approaches focusing on the smallest units of sound rather than the larger units of meaning. But let us reserve judgement until we have found out more.

To bring all of this to life here is an example cited by Freire which makes it more vivid.

> . . . we visited a Culture Circle in a small fishing community called Monte Mario. They had as a generative word the term *bonito* (beautiful), the name of a fish, and as a codification they had an expressive design of the little town with its vegetation, typical houses, fishing boats in the sea, and a fisherman holding a *bonito*. The learners were looking at this codification in silence. All at once, four of them stood up as if they had agreed to do so beforehand; and they walked over to the wall where the codification was hanging. They stared at the codification closely. Then they went to the window and looked outside. They looked at each other as though they were surprised and looking again at the codification, they said: 'This is Monte Mario. Monte Mario is like this and we didn't know it'. (Freire and Macedo 1987: xxi)

A rather surprising response and Freire's analysis is that it was only the routine followed by the organisers which had enabled the participants to engage in a fundamental act of mind, namely, *recognition*. Recognition is an everyday word familiar to us all and the process of recognition is essential to learning, to reading the world and to reading words. What is interesting here is how close Freire's thinking is to that of another great educationalist, Jerome Bruner. He said that recognition – knowing what something is – requires more than being able to say what a thing is. It requires consideration of what a thing might be. In order to recognise something one has to draw on memory, on physical exploration (looking, touching and so on), comparing, categorising and naming. My mother tells the story of how, when I was a small child, I was taken to the docks in the small seaside town of East London in South Africa. There I came across some of the metal structures that boats are tied to. I had never seen one before so I did what all small children do – set out to find out what it was. I finally announced 'I seed it and I feeled it and it is not a dog'. This encapsulates the process of recognition and naming – although I was too young to be able to explore the function of the object.

The methods developed by Freire in Brazil in the early 1960s for native language literacy are still in use in many developing countries in Latin America and Africa. In the United States, organisations such as the Hispanic Literacy Council in Chicago; Bronx Educational Services, Union Settlement House, El Barrio Popular and the Amalgamated Clothing and Textile Workers Union in New York; BASE in Los Angeles and the Adult Literacy Resources Institute in Boston have used Freire's methods to teach initial literacy in Spanish, in what are sometimes referred to as Basic Education in the Native Language (BENL) programmes. But there are critics and we will come to them in due course.

Another way of looking

Moacir Gadotti (1994), who has written a book on the life and work of Freire, explains what happens in the culture circles in a much more approachable way. He talks about *literacy and conscientization* and explains the stages of Freire's pedagogy like this:

A person, called an alphabetizer, using a notebook or tape recorder, worked with groups of people, recording everything heard or read with the aim of making a list of all the words used by the people. Words and phrases, expressions, particular ways of speaking or talking about the world, the words of songs and rhymes were all recorded. What emerged in each circle were the problems experienced in the everyday lives of the group. The list of words was then analysed to pick out generative words which were chosen both for their meaning and relevance to the group according to the need for them to represent all the phonemes of Portuguese. Gadotti calls this first phase the *Investigation Stage*.

Gadotti calls the second stage the *Thematization Stage* and this involves the process of codifying and decodifying. Codifying is essentially a way of representing aspects of the lives of the group which have emerged in the first stage. To illustrate how this might work let's take the word *labourers* as an example. The generative themes which could emerge from this might include different kinds of work/labour, political and economic power, different wages for different work, conditions and pay. So the process might look something like this:

The group might talk about the value of work – theirs and that of others and the rewards available. Questions arising might include how much certain types of workers are paid; if this is fair and just; what wages are spent on and are they adequate to the life needs of the workers; what laws govern wages; what about working conditions like days off, holiday, bonuses and conditions. All of this is said to arise from the ways in which the generative word is codified. If, for example, the first codification of labourers is a picture of a farm the discussion might at first focus on farm labour but would almost certainly extend to talking about other workers.

The last stage is called the *Problematization Stage* and this is the stage where the focus shifts to enabling the members of the group initially to learn the skills of reading and writing to enable them to become instruments of struggle able not only to question but to find ways of changing society.

Functional literacy, domesticating literacy

You may well have heard people talking about *functional literacy* and the precise meaning of this term has changed over time. Initially, enabling illiterate people in the developing world to become able to read and write in order to be able to function in society was just that. Over time this approach has come to be seen as minimalist since the word 'function' suggests something mechanical rather than human. Jonathan Kozol (1991) rejected the term saying that using functional literacy as a goal reduces people to the status of objects. All that they need is the acquisition of low-level skills which will enable them to function in the work place rather than critically participate in it and in other aspects of their lives. His work is both interesting and relevant and has a focus on inequality in education in the United States.

On a different but related issue Kenneth Levine believed that traditional definitions of functional literacy place more emphasis on reading than on writing and it is his view that writing is the thing more likely to bring about change. A person who can write can express on paper and to an audience her ideas, thoughts, fear, beliefs, values and has more chance to change views. It would suit many societies to keep the huge numbers of illiterate adults still evident throughout the world subdued and contained. In Levine's terms the effect would be 'to domesticate and further subordinate rather than to increase the autonomy and social standing of the previously illiterate person' (Levine 1986: 41).

By now you will have realised that all of Freire's work was underpinned by a strongly held belief in the importance of literacy and learning to the emancipation of people. For him everything to do with learning and literacy was political. He was working with adults and it is clear that both the materials offered the students in terms of reading materials and the way in which they were taught would let us decide if the aims of the educators were to promote critical literacy, functional literacy or domesticating literacy. Let's move to the world of early childhood for a contrast or a parallel.

The intersection between the work of Paulo Freire and the world of early childhood development

In one sense children who are becoming literate in this country are extremely fortunate because there are so many books written in English which can be described as books to think with. Many of them are picture books where both image and text carry a story – sometimes two different stories. Many of them are about the themes that obsess and concern children – loss, death, the dark, friendships, being different, loneliness and grief, for example. Young children who are fortunate enough to encounter these books are being offered opportunities to develop the ability to reflect on and question their world. In other words children are being offered opportunities to develop critical literacy. You may want to contrast books like this with the sort of primers offered in some schools where the focus is almost entirely on enabling children to decode words rather than read for meaning.

In recent years, however, there has been a trend to move from a dialogic approach, to a narrower one with an emphasis on the building blocks of the written language rather than on the making and sharing of meaning. In all schools you will find much of the school day devoted to getting children to use the smallest building blocks of language (the sounds) rather than the essential building blocks of meaning.

In the next chapter you can find an account of how an inner-city primary school in London, serving a richly diverse community, developed a programme to promote literacy. This was based on recognising the significance of communication, the power of literacy, the need to include parents and children in what was planned. It was based on the work of people like Margaret Meek, Myra Barrs and others and during its time was seen as very positive. At the same time many young children were being encouraged to become writers and to use whatever means available to them to put their ideas on paper. Known as emergent writing it fell out of favour, just as reading for meaning fell out of favour. Here are examples of emergent writing which come from Glenda Bissex's (1984) influential book about how her son, Paul, became a writer. The wonderful title of the book is:

GNYS AT WRK.

See if you can get the meaning from each one.
When Paul was 5 years old he wrote a message for his mum like this:

YDUDT

To decode this you might need to know that Paul used these approaches: when a word sounds like the name of a letter, he uses that letter, so Y equals why, U equals you; he sometimes uses the first letter of a word, sometimes the last. He has a system. His question above is "Why did you do it?"
Six months later Paul wrote:

WN U ST I GT SD

Paul has elaborated his system so he sometimes uses the first and last letters of a word and he knows that in order for something to be read there must be spaces between words. This one says 'When you shout I get sad'.

Any child, trying to make sense of the world in all its facets, develops a theory and tries it out. Each time she does something someone responds and the response helps her know if she is on the right track. No one gives her lessons. She is actively watching, listening, questioning, trying, watching, listening, questioning, trying. The child – not yet a reader or a writer is not yet literate, so in some ways is similar to the adults in Freire's group who, one must assume, would like to be able to watch, listen, question and try.

Looking back, looking ahead

In this chapter we have examined some of Freire's thinking about the importance of learning to understand, transform and critique our world as precursors of being able to speak, read and write words and text. There has been much to grapple with in this chapter but many of the themes addressed here are revisited throughout the book. In the next chapter we look in more detail at his ideas on the philosophy and the politics of literacy illustrated and supported by a number of examples, anecdotes, quotations and case studies.

Chapter 5

The definition, philosophy and politics of literacy

We have now defined some terms, looked at some aspects of Freire's life and begun to consider some of the ideas he developed and sharpened over the course of a long and full life. In this chapter we stay with the subject of literacy – which was, after all, one of the key themes in his life – and examine more closely just what he believed particularly in terms of literacy and *oppression*. Here we draw on some individual experiences and make links with the work of Lev Vygotsky. You will find things which have already been touched on being elaborated here.

Education and oppression

You may feel a little surprised to find the words *education* and *oppression* in the same sentence. What can one have to do with the other? I grew up in South Africa during the terrible apartheid years. I was the child of educated middle-class immigrant parents and that was enough to ensure that I had access to all the privileges available to those with white skin. I was part of the privileged minority. Under apartheid, as you must know, the minority white people ruled the country, held the wealth and the power, made and implemented the rules. They developed parallel programmes of education – one for white children and one for black children. We were all supposed to be educated according to what the government of the day thought we could both achieve and contribute to the country. As a white child I could hope to become a teacher, a doctor, a musician, a lawyer – anything I dreamed of. But a black child of the same age could hope only to become barely functionally literate and to be equipped to be a cleaner, a labourer and only possibly a very low-grade teacher. The education system was set up to maintain the status quo, adding more privilege to the already fortunate, and oppressing, silencing and domesticating the rest.

After the extraordinary collapse of the apartheid system the nation called itself the rainbow nation and, under the leadership of Nelson Mandela, set about building a free and equal society. But the effects of the apartheid system were long-lasting and affected not only those who had been oppressed but also the oppressors. Those who had held the power, the wealth and the privileges never saw that having all these rights was anything other than their just deserts. They talked about their better education, their greater efforts, their superior skills which entitled them to have these privileges and blamed those who were oppressed as being inadequate, inferior, stupid, ungrateful and envious. In Freire's terms the oppressors had, in effect, been as dehumanised as those they have oppressed.

> Any situation in which 'A' objectively exploits 'B' or hinders his and her pursuit of self-affirmation as a responsible person is one of oppression. Such a situation in itself constitutes violence, even when sweetened by false generosity, because it interferes with the individual's ontological and historical vocation to be more fully human. With the establishment of a relationship of oppression, violence has already begun. Never in history has violence been initiated by the oppressed. How could they be the initiators, if they themselves are the result of violence? How could they be the sponsors of something whose objective inauguration called forth their existence as oppressed? There would be no oppressed had there been no prior situation of violence to establish their subjection. (Freire 1996: 37)

Apartheid offers an extreme and overt example but South Africa was certainly not the only country whose educational system had been publicly and proudly designed to keep things as they are and pay no attention to redressing inequality or eradicating oppression. Look around you and ask if you can find examples here, where you live.

Freire is most famous for the first book he wrote, *Pedagogy of the Oppressed*, which was initially published in Portuguese in 1968 and in English two years later. The book is dedicated like this:

> To the oppressed
> and to those who suffer with them
> and fight at their side.

The intersection between the work of Paulo Freire and the world of early childhood development

Pedagogy of the Oppressed and a school in Hackney

I first read the book about nine years after it was published in English, when I was working in an inner London primary school where there were (and still are) many children whose parents were immigrants, speakers of languages other than

English and often not literate. As a school we were working hard to promote literacy and had established a way of teaching young children to read by using real picture and story books, reading aloud to them often and encouraging them to retell the stories. The old reading scheme books were relegated to a cupboard and we raised money to buy high-quality children's literature. We spent as much of our budget as we could employing primary helpers (now called teaching assistants) and tried to ensure that some could speak our community languages. They were all involved in our daily reading session. Slowly we noticed that what we were doing was working. Children were choosing to look at and read books and wanted to take them home. We then invited parents to come in if they were able and to either be part of a group listening to a story being read aloud or to tell a story to the children. We got some parents to translate some of the books into the languages of their homes so we made our own dual text books. In these situations they were the experts and we the learners. We got parents to actually write and illustrate books for their own children. There were obvious problems and we were certainly not reaching everybody. But what we were doing was building a culture of literacy in the school. Books mattered: narrative mattered; everyone had the potential to be a story maker and a story sharer. And we were building mutual respect. So Freire's arguments really spoke to me and I recommended the book to everyone I met. It was one of the seminal books in my working life.

Freire was absolutely clear that education can never be neutral. It either keeps people where they are in the sense of not inviting them to become thinkers and problem solvers or it liberates them. In the famous preschools established by Loris Malaguzzi in Reggio Emilia there is an explicit aim which is to build a pedagogy of relationships, of questioning and of respect. There is a clear emphasis on enabling all children to use not only literacy in terms of words, but literacy in terms of the arts, music, making, constructing and much more. In other words young children are invited to use a hundred languages or myriad ways of expressing their thoughts and ideas. Freire would have described this as an approach to building an education that was *humanising*, liberating and *emancipatory*. And what about literacy? Where does that fit in? Our society is a print society where almost every aspect of education depends on being literate in the sense of being able to read and write. Where an educational system allows only the few to become both literate *and* critical it is a system which maintains oppression and inequality.

It is important, too, to remember that all human beings have a history which means that we are all conscious of time and of where we are in time. We all have a past, a present and a future. As a result we are conscious of cause and effect and how we, human beings, have lived together in groups and made things and systems together in our groups. We have developed tools to help us both control and describe our world: we have made things to show our feelings about the world and the people in it. At the time of writing there is an amazing exhibition on at the British Museum showing the extraordinary pieces of art made by human beings as long as 40,000 years ago. We see people just like us, with brains like ours, making objects and marks to represent both their world and their emotions.

Thinking about culture and cultural tools

I want here to introduce some of the most important ideas of Lev Vygotsky, the great Russian theorist who died young but in whose work I find some overlap with the work of Freire, particularly with regard to what makes us human. Vygotsky examined human development from a *sociohistorical perspective*, just as we are finding that Freire did. He was very interested in language, just as Freire was, although his interest was in the cognitive aspects of language acquisition and use whereas Freire was interested in analysing language and linking it to equity: a more political and linguistic perspective. It was clear that both context and culture were important for Vygotsky.

Cultural tools are devices humans use for mastering their thinking and problem solving. They are not natural but artificial (by which we mean created by humans) and they have come about through social rather than individual actions. Among the things that Vygotsky defined as cultural tools are these: language; systems of counting; mnemonic devices; symbols including algebraic and musical symbols; works of art; writing; diagrams; maps; road signs and so on. Can you see how each of these has come about through the efforts of people working in groups or societies and have come about as ways of refining thinking and helping solve problems?

- We have developed a system of symbols to represent numbers. This enables us to use a kind of shorthand to represent our thinking. So if we need to work out how many objects we have if we have 10 groups of 5 objects we can express this as $10 \times 5 = 50$ and don't have to lay out 10 groups with 5 objects in each.
- If we need to go from our own home to another place this is made simpler if we have a representational and diagrammatic plan to help us. So we use a map.

- Our culture has developed a system of road signs in order to ensure that drivers and cyclists and pedestrians can travel more safely by knowing what is ahead of them, what is permissible and what is not.

Cultural tools are the products of human cultural and historical activity. Pea (1993) says that these tools literally carry intelligence in them, in that they represent some individual's or some community's decision that the means thus offered – the cultural tools – would make life better for individuals or groups. He added that as the tools become so familiar as to be almost invisible it gets harder to see them 'carrying' intelligence. He says that what we see is that intelligence lies with the person who is using the tools. Cole (1996) suggests that cultural tools should be considered a subcategory of the overarching notion of artefact – where artefacts are defined as objects created by man (sic). People and objects can both act as mediating artefacts.

In all cultures throughout the world people have developed ways of representing their thoughts and feelings through using symbolic means like writing, painting, music and dance. Vygotsky was insistent that humans become aware of their own thoughts through and with these tools. The question is often asked 'Can you think without language?' and although responses to this differ it seems clear that most of us believe that we need some additional tool (drawing, painting, music, symbols, language) in order to make clear to ourselves (which is how we might define 'thinking') what we are thinking or contemplating. Freire would talk of this as becoming conscious and this access to analysing or questioning or explaining implies understanding not only what is good and right but also what is unfair and wrong. Vygotsky would have argued the following:

1. The individual is an active agent in the process.
2. Everything takes place within a context where the individual uses the tools which are available at that time and in that place.

In naming, reading and writing the world we use and create cultural tools. Think of the role of spoken and written language; about how in codifying or representing situations we might use paintings or drawings or photographs; in communicating our thoughts we might use word processors, typewriters, keyboards, pens and pencils. All of this takes place within the contexts of real life, so within families or communities or work places or schools or colleges. Culture and context are significant to our lives and our needs. We have seen how Freire felt able to analyse words on the basis of syllables, possible within the language of Portuguese but less so within other languages.

Let's summarise Vygotsky's thoughts on cultural tools as follows:

- When a tool is developed it allows for the development of several new functions connected with the use of the tool and its control.
- When a tool is developed it allows several natural processes to die out since the tool now accomplishes the work done by these processes. This means that thinking becomes more efficient, more complex and quicker.
- The whole structure of behaviour is changed in the same way that the development of material tools (hammers, computers, for example) changes the whole structure of physical or labour tasks (drawn from Smidt 2008).

Being illiterate

Those of you reading this are, by definition, able to read. Can you imagine what it feels like not to be able to read? Can you put yourself in the shoes of people who are in this position and imagine how dehumanised, under-valued, worthless they might feel? The comments gathered here have come from a variety of sources, from workshops in South Africa, quotations from famous people (cited online) and students studying *Language and Power* in London.

- Savita said: 'It is very hard for me and I feel shame that I can't read. I won't go to my little boy's school when they ask me to – my husband has to go – because I am scared that they will think I am stupid or lazy. They send home books from the school for me to read with my little boy and I just tell him to tell me the story or look at the pictures. I am scared that the teachers, if they know I can't read, will give up on my boy and not help him learn to read'. (Personal communication)
  Savita is absolutely clear about how being unable to read affects her life and potentially her relationships with her child, her husband and the school. She fears that her inability will reflect on her as a mother and as a human being. Is she right?
- Bertold Brecht said: 'The worst illiterate is the political illiterate, he doesn't hear, doesn't speak, nor participate in the political events. He doesn't know the cost of life, the price of the bean, of the fish, of the flour, of the rent, of the shoes and of the medicine, all depends on political decisions. The political illiterate is so stupid that he is proud and swells his chest saying that he hates politics. The imbecile doesn't know that, from his political ignorance is born the prostitute, the abandoned child, and the worst thieves of all, the bad politician, corrupted and

flunky of the national and multinational companies'. (www.goodreads.
com/quotes/tag/illiteracy)
A devastating appraisal of illiteracy and ignorance and its potential
consequences.

- Primo Levi, writing about the concentration camps, said: 'The experi-
mental character of the camps is clear to us today and arouses an intense
retrospective horror. We know now that the German camps, whether
intended for work or for extermination, were not, so to speak, a by-
product of conditions of national emergency (the Nazi revolution first,
then the war). They were not an unfortunate transitory necessity, but
the early seedlings of the New Order. In the New Order, some human
races (Jews, gypsies) would be wiped out while others, for example the
Slavs in general and the Russians in particular, would be enslaved and
subject to a carefully controlled regime of biological degradation, transforming individuals into good labouring animals, illiterate, devoid of
all initiative, incapable of either rebellion or criticism'. (www.primolevi.
it/Web/English/Contents/Auschwitz/100_Arbeit_macht_frei/«Arbeit_
macht_frei»,_by_Primo_Levi)
- Mary Karr: 'Childhood was terrifying for me. A kid has no control.
You're three feet tall, flat broke, unemployed, and illiterate. Terror snaps
you awake. You pay keen attention. People can just pick you up and
move you and put you down. One of my favorite poems, by Nicanor
Parra, is called "Memories of Youth": "All I'm sure of is that I kept going
back and forth./Sometimes I bumped into trees,/bumped into beggars./I
forced my way through a thicket of chairs and tables." Our little cracker
box of a house could give you the adrenaline rush of fear, which means
more frames of memory per second. Emotional memories are stored deep
in the snake brain, which is probably why aphasics in nursing homes
often cuss so much – that language doesn't erode in a stroke'. (www.
theparisreview.org/interviews/5992/the-art-of-memoir-no-1-mary-karr)
Mary Karr, the poet, compares being illiterate to being a child. Both are
powerless.
- Alberto Manguel in *The History of Reading* said: 'As centuries of dicta-
tors have known, an illiterate crowd is the easiest to rule; since the craft
of reading cannot be untaught once it has been acquired, the second-best
recourse is to limit its scope'. (www.goodreads.com/quotes/tag/illiteracy)
Manguel makes an important point – the political power claimed by
those who keep other people oppressed and illiterate.
- Siswe, attending an adult literacy class, said: 'When you can't read you not
only feel stupid but you are stupid because the only voice you hear is your
own. I know that my life is miserable and that I am not treated fairly but
I don't know what I can do to change things'. (Student interview notes)

Siswe reminds us of how, through reading the words of others, we are not completely alone.

- Kofi Annan said: 'Literacy is a bridge from misery to hope. It is a tool for daily life in modern society. It is a bulwark against poverty, and a building block of development, an essential complement to investments in roads, dams, clinics and factories. Literacy is a platform for democratization, and a vehicle for the promotion of cultural and national identity. Especially for girls and women, it is an agent of family health and nutrition. For everyone, everywhere, literacy is, along with education in general, a basic human right. . . . Literacy is, finally, the road to human progress and the means through which every man, woman and child can realize his or her full potential'. (www.goodreads.com/quotes/113611-literacy-is-a-bridge-from-misery-to-hope-it-is)
  I love the idea that literacy is a bridge from misery to hope and a tool for daily life.
- Melissande from Mali said: 'My daughter can't go to school. She started but now it is difficult and only boys can go. I want to teach her to read but there are no books so we are making words by writing in the dust or with our fingers on the window. She will be able to do this but she will not be able to go far enough. They will keep her and all the girls just as ignorant women to have babies and look after the home. I want my daughter to be able to think for herself'. (Personal communication)
  The recent troubles in Mali have changed opportunities for women and girls to access education and, by implication, literacy. Melissande is well aware of the dreadful consequences for individuals and society.
- Greg Mortenson (2010), in his book *Stones into Schools: Promoting Peace with Books, not Bombs, in Afghanistan and Pakistan*, said: 'They are a testament not only to the Afghans' hunger for literacy, but also to their willingness to pour scarce resources into this effort, even during a time of war. I have seen children studying in classrooms set up inside animal sheds, windowless basements, garages, and even an abandoned public toilet. We ourselves have run schools out of refugee tents, shipping containers, and the shells of bombed-out Soviet armored personnel carriers. The thirst for education over there is limitless. The Afghans want their children to go to school because literacy represents what neither we nor anyone else has so far managed to offer them: hope, progress, and the possibility of controlling their own destiny.' (http://startthesound.blogspot.co.uk/p/rachaels-quotes.html)
  A humanitarian speaker and writer's analysis of what literacy means in terms of hope, progress and destiny particularly for war-torn Afghanistan and divided Pakistan.

Teaching literacy to adults

Here are two case studies of approaches to teaching literacy to adults used in different places and at different times. Read each one carefully and decide which, if either, represents functional literacy and which liberatory literacy.

Case study 1: competency in literacy for adults

The local council decided it was important to offer some help to the large numbers of illiterate adults living in the borough. Their initial focus was on two things they felt would be essential to ensuring that their cohort could become sufficiently literate to cope with daily life: *content and skills*. Content refers to what the students should learn and this was based on what the council decided illiterate people would need to know and included knowing the value of the money in their pockets; what jobs they might be able to do; how to find out about the resources in their area; how to contact a doctor or other health worker, and what rights they have in law. By skills they meant the four traditional communication skills of reading, writing, speaking and listening; ability to use a computer and access the Internet; solving simple real-life problems and interpersonal skills. They then defined what the learners would have to demonstrate they could do within the content and skills which would allow the programme developers to say that any learner had achieved the defined targets.

Just to give you the flavour of the types of targets they set, here are a number. As you read each one say if you think achieving this target might help the learners feel as though their life chances are as good as those of others or if they will merely be slightly better able at coping with continuing adversity.

1.1. Can fill in a job application form after reading the job advert in the local paper;
1.2. Can count out the required number of notes and coins to purchase something in a shop;
1.3. Can follow a recipe including being able to weigh items.

(Loosely based on Sticht and Armstrong, Adult Performance Level Study, 1975, www.nald.ca/library/research/adlitus/adlitus.pdf)

Case study 2: using photographs to develop consciousness and the ability to criticise

Boal (2000) wrote about a project involving a theatre group in Latin America which used photography as a tool to enable illiterate adults to discover, describe and critique things in their everyday lives. They wanted to enable the participants to discuss the enormous problems daily life presented to them and to share the problems and explore any solutions. Each participant was given a simple camera and taught how to use it. They were asked to use the camera to answer the question to illustrate or give some impression of where they live. They set off with the cameras, took their photographs and returned to share them with the group. The aim was for them to convey something about their lives – which were filled with difficulties – and to find links between their experiences.

- The first picture shown was of the interior of a shack made of straw mats and consisting of only one room. It is common in Lima where the picture was taken for a family to live in one room. Here everything is exposed and visible. You can imagine how many issues this photograph raised.
- The second photograph was of the bank of the river known to all in the group. It floods regularly and life on the banks is very dangerous and many children drown in it.
- Another photograph showed the face of a child covered in blood. One member of the group questioned the person who had taken this photograph since it did not seem to show where he lived. His response was:

Look at his face: there is blood on it. This child, as all the others who live here, have their lives threatened by the rats that infest the whole bank of the river Rimac. They are protected by dogs that attack the rats and scare them away. But there was a mange epidemic and the city dog-catcher came around here catching lots of dogs and taking them away. This child had a dog who protected him. During the day his parents used to go to work and he was left with his dog. But now he doesn't have it any more. A few days ago, when you asked me where I lived, the rats had come while the child was sleeping and had eaten part of his nose . . . Look at this picture; it is my answer. I live in a place where things like this still happen. (Boal 2000: 124)

Analysing those two very different ways of teaching illiterate and poor adults, what did you feel? Could you describe one approach as adopting a top-down approach and the other a more dialogic one? Even though these are crudely drawn it is quite clear that the first one adopts a traditional and top-down approach with the educators as experts deciding what the participants need, whereas the second relies on a proper dialogue between educators and learners. The learners in the first model have no opportunity to say what it is they want to learn or how they want their lives to be changed. Would you agree that the first model illustrates an attempt to achieve functional literacy and the second that of working towards emancipatory literacy?

The intersection between the work of Paulo Freire and the world of early childhood development

At a UNESCO Conference in Paris in 2008 the issue of the role of early childhood education in sustainable societies was debated and a book produced detailing some of the presentations. One of these came from Lenira Haddad who was writing about what was happening with regards to early childhood education in her home country of Brazil.

At the time of writing, Brazil was, like many developing countries, in the process of trying to bring early childhood education provision closer to the provision of compulsory schooling. This started with the approval of the *Law of Guidelines and Bases of National Education* which recognises early childhood education as the first step in basic education and unifies the service, and, in the process, generates some rules and regulations governing things like the qualifications for early childhood education professionals. This approach is making its way through the country and bringing with it both advantages and disadvantages. As you can imagine the disadvantages are in making preschools more like primary schools rather than making primary schools become more like nursery classes. So the Brazilians are finding that features like times of opening, levels of staffing, adult-child ratios and isolation from child welfare, health and related services are less family-friendly and less child-centred.

Haddad discusses the *specific dignity* of early childhood education which she sees as an essential part of achieving a sustainable society. What she means is that as early childhood education becomes an important system in its own right with its own identity, it must become able to open up dialogue between the needs of civil society and the resources available for children and their families. Discussion needs to include the issues around gender roles, the balance between family and working life, the upbringing of children who spend some time beyond the traditional boundaries of family life and the everyday and intense relationships that characterise the volatile emotional lives of young children. The issue is that old paradigms need to be challenged if this special dignity is to be achieved. I wonder if you feel we need a similar debate in this country.

You may be asking what all of this has to do with the ideas of Freire. For Freire one of the problems with schooling was the nondialogic nature of the pedagogy. As Brazil increasingly adopts the *schoolifying* model for preschools there is the huge risk that there will be more of a top-down approach with the curriculum being decided remotely and not in dialogue; and children being taught formally rather than through play, exploration, questioning and the use of their hundred languages. The roles of parents and family will become less and less central and, says Haddad, this will 'contaminate our early childhood system. Millions of children all over the world, especially from poor families, instead of appropriate early childhood pedagogy, will experience pedagogy for submission'. (2008: 36)

This is serious stuff and certainly not limited to Brazil. You have only to look at the demands made of young children in our schooling system to see this in action.

Looking back, looking ahead

This chapter has taken a slightly different format in that it is made up largely of examples and case studies. This is to consolidate what has already been said in order to ensure that you understand just what Freire was addressing when he developed his model of dialogic teaching. And this is where we go in the next two chapters.

Chapter 6

Part 1: what kind of teaching and learning do we want?

This is the first of two chapters which lie at the heart of this book. Here we examine what is known as *banking education* and examine the effect it has on both learners and teachers. Much of this might be familiar to you from your own experiences as a learner or teacher, parent or practitioner. As usual some key terms will be defined (remember to check in the glossary). They will often be analysed and examples will be drawn involving sometimes very young children and sometimes adults.

Defining terms: dialogue and problem-posing

Dialogue is an everyday word with which you will be familiar. In the context of Freire's work dialogue is defined very specifically to mean the relationships between two (or more) *knowledgeable equals* in a situation of *two-way communication.* You will see that the phrases knowledgeable equals and two-way communication are italicised. That is because they are particularly significant to our understanding of dialogue and dialogic education.

Here are two examples of teaching and learning situations for young children. You decide which, if either, fit Freire's definition. To arrive at a conclusion, what questions would you ask as you read the examples?

Tala and Emily writing

Charmian Kenner looked at what some six-year-old bilingual children were doing at a Community Saturday School where they were learning to write in their home/family language whilst continuing to learn literacy in English at their primary school. *Peer teaching* sessions were set up so that the children could teach one another how to write in Chinese or Arabic or Spanish—three languages with very different *graphic systems.* Here is some of what happened when Tala tried to teach Emily to write a word in Arabic—a language with which Emily was not familiar. Tala wanted to teach Emily to write her brother's name, Khalid. This is written in two parts, 'Kha' and 'lid' because, according to the rules of Arabic writing, the letters 'alif' (which represent the 'a' sound) cannot join to any following letter. Tala wrote the word herself, in front of Emily, telling her what she was doing.

> '. . . Do that – it's like a triangle, but it's got a line like here . . . go "wheee" like this' (as she finished with an upward stroke). Emily tried to follow this lead, saying as she wrote 'It looks like an "L" . . . it looks like steps'. . . . Emily was interpreting an unfamiliar script from the basis of English and of visual images. However, Tala realized that Emily had over-interpreted her instructions, with the result being too stylized and she commented 'It's not exactly like that – she's done steps'. Indeed, Emily's version looked like steps in a staircase rather than the fluid curves typical of Arabic writing. This difficulty continued during the lesson and to help her friend produce more appropriate writing, Tala resorted to a technique used by her own Arabic teacher. She provided a 'join-the-dots' version of the words required. (Kenner 2004: 113)

Class B learning 'ing'

The teacher is standing in front of the year 1 class where the children are only a year or two older than the children in the previous example. She has written the letters 'ing' on the board. She starts the lesson by telling the children, who are seated on the carpet, that they will be looking at endings of words and that they will be looking especially at what she calls 'doing words'. She asks the children who can tell her what a doing word is. Several hands go up and a child is chosen, offers the word 'verb' and is praised. The teacher then asks the children who can tell her what the letters 'ing' say. The lesson progresses in this way until the children are each given a work sheet and asked to draw a picture of each of the verbs written on it. (Personal observation notes)

I wonder what questions you had in your mind as you tried to assess these examples in terms of being dialogic or not. They are so crudely different that the task was simple, but asking you to raise questions was trying to put you in the position of being dialogic in order for you to be able to be critical. The most obvious questions to ask were if the teacher and learners in each example were equal partners and whether there was genuine two-way communication between the players.

You will have had no difficulty in seeing the differences between the two examples. In the first it is clear that the teacher knows, recognises and appreciates that children can have knowledge of aspects of their own lives and culture that the teacher does not have. Tala knew much more about the conventions of writing Arabic words because this was part of her culture and experience. By inviting one knowledgeable child to teach the other children about something indicates an awareness on the part of the teacher that everyone has experience which gives them knowledge and expertise that others might not have. In doing this the teacher does not make this true for only one child but recognises that all children are knowledgeable but about different things. Here the teacher sets up a situation which is dialogic in the sense that all those participating are seen as equal and the situation invites the asking and answering of questions. There is dialogue between the participants and the situation can be described as *problem-posing*. The problem posed in this case was how to help Emily be able to make the more fluid marks required to resemble those of Arabic scripts.

By contrast the second example clearly has the teacher in the position of expert, holder of knowledge and in control whilst the children are passive, required only to answer questions raised by the teacher. When they move on to working independently they are being asked to all do the same thing at the same time rather than be able to draw on their own individual and unique experience. There is no sense of dialogue.

This leads us to the second word to be defined, although it has already been used. This is the word *problem-posing*. This has nothing to do with problem solving or the skills required to solve problems which are terms used often in education. For Freire problem-posing is essential to real dialogue and is deeply embedded in culture and context. For the teacher and the learner to be equals in the dialogue each has to know about the lives, interests and concerns of the other. The teacher can only operate as an equal partner when she knows what it is that the learner is interested in, concerned about, paying attention to, asking questions about. Those of us involved in the care and education of young children know this well and it very often informs our thinking and our work.

The intersection between the work of Paulo Freire and the world of early childhood development

Read the examples which follow to decide which suggests the teacher is genuinely concerned with knowing about the context and culture of the learners. Decide too which seem to you to be examples of problem-posing.

Wataru is a spinner

Wataru was 14 months old at the time of the observation. He had just started at day care. One day he approached one of the teachers with a circular plastic ring in his hand. The teacher took the ring and spun it on the floor with her fingers. The child imitated the adult's actions, but not successfully. He then put the ring on the table and tried to spin it there. It did spin a little. Later he crawled away leaving the ring on the floor but returned a little later with a ring with a large diameter. He crawled with the ring in front of him to show the teacher and he held it in the air to get her attention. She did not do anything with the ring at first but offered the child another toy which he ignored. The teacher made the big ring spin and Wataru took the small ring and succeeded in getting it to spin. At which point he hooted with delight. Still later he found a white tray which was circular and tried to get it to spin and when he was successful the teacher clapped her hands to confirm his success. Later still, a little girl picked up the tray and ran off with it. Wataru tried to run after her but could not. The little girl teased him with the tray. A few days later he had a ring in his hand and the teacher had a tray and they were sitting in front of a mirror. He started spinning the ring on the floor with great skill and then moved on to spinning the tray. Later he managed to get a thick wooden ring to spin too.

The learning process started with Wataru imitating the teacher spinning a plastic ring he had given her on her finger. It was his evident passion for spinning things that made him persist in his search for answers to his unvoiced questions. On the basis of trial and error and watching what others did, he was able to compile a mental list of 'spinnable' objects. (Smidt 2013: 124)

Louisa loves circles

In another nursery three-year-old Louisa is obsessed with circles and rotation. Using pens or crayons she draws circles on paper; with a stick she draws circles in the dust; with her finger she draws them on the misty window pane. Outside she turns round and round or runs around waving her arms in circular motion as she goes. If she is choosing to make something out of collage materials she shows a determined preference for circles. Her teacher has noticed this and ensures that she offers this little girl many opportunities to encounter and work with circles and rotation. She understands that repeated patterns of action are serious attempts to make sense of the world. (Observation made by a student teacher)

Maths in the classroom

Giulio is very interested in numbers. He takes notice of them and pays attention to how they work. He often says things in class—things that are unusual and draw the attention of a student teacher doing her teaching practice in his class. Here are some of the comments he made and questions he raised:

'I wonder why the numbers on the houses don't go 1, 2, 3, 4. On our side of the road they go 6, 8, 10 and on the other side they go 5, 7, 9. My dad says those are odd numbers and I think it is odd that they don't work the way proper numbers do'.

'If you count in 5s the last number is always 5 or 0. I wonder why'.

The class teacher, however, intent on getting through her maths lesson each day, groups the children into ability groups and regards Giulio as being a noisy child who constantly comes up with what she calls 'irrelevant comments'. If you pay attention to what this child is noting and asking you will realise just how thoughtful and curious he is. In the class each group is given a worksheet related to their perceived levels of ability and the teacher works with a different group each day. When the student teacher asked why Giulio was not in the 'top' group she was told that it was because he mucks around doing his own thing and never gets to finish the required work.

In the first two examples the children are showing evidence of repeated patterns of action. Wataru spins everything he can and Louisa makes and uses circles. Piaget talked of this *schematic behaviour* as being cognitively significant and it is clear that children doing it are engaged in posing one or more problems or asking questions which they are trying to solve. The teachers of the young children concerned are aware of this and in their responses and planning take proper and respectful account of it. Contrast that with the class teacher's inability to pay close attention to Giulio's really interesting questions. Pressure of work, a programme to follow and boxes to be ticked take precedence.

Think back to what you read about how Freire trained his coordinators to be able to work dialogically. Do you remember how much time they spent in gathering information about individual culture groups? How they listened to what the learners were saying and then codified this in some way to make it visual before moving on to the task of teaching those adults to read? They were being asked to do exactly what good early years workers are trained to do—find out as much as possible about the child and her prior experience, interests, fears, the languages of her home, her position in the family and much more. Later, when working with the children, they are trained to watch and listen and think about what it is the children are doing as they play. They are trained also to notice what questions (spoken or implied) the children are asking as they engage in what sometimes appears to be random behaviour.

Banking education

It was in *Pedagogy of the Oppressed* that Freire spelled out the differences between banking and dialogic education. He started by looking at what he called the *narrative nature* of the relationship between the teacher and the students. As you know, the word *narrative* means story so the narrative nature means the story-like behaviour. The teacher, who is the active agent in any situation where banking education is taking place, is the one holding the power. She tells the narrative to the passive, powerless and patient learners. The narrative might go like this: 'The capital city of Afghanistan is Kabul' or like this 'two times four is eight'. In each and every case the teacher tells the story about aspects of reality as though they were static, predictable and often beyond the experiential understanding of the students. From the first of those two statements the child learns nothing at all about either Kabul or Afghanistan—nothing about the wars that have raged there, the way women and girls are treated, the foods that are eaten, the types of houses that are built. All the learner can do is memorise and then present or change the factual statement. How many of us learned 'two twos are four, three twos are six' and so on? And did we understand what twice two or thrice two meant?

Freire's analysis was that in situations like these the students were treated like empty vessels being filled up with facts or bits of knowledge by the teacher. In many classrooms and other educational settings the teacher is depositing her hard-won and seemingly valuable knowledge in the empty vessels which constitute the brains of the learners, just as she might deposit her salary in the bank. Such knowledge is seen as 'the property of the teacher rather than a medium evoking the critical reflection of both teacher and students' (Freire 1996: 61). In this system, where education becomes an act of depositing something which is often meaningless to the learner in her brain, and giving orders and instructions, the learner remains merely and passively accepting, memorising and repeating. She cannot ask questions, make links with her own reality by drawing on her own experience or contribute her thoughts and ideas. This is the banking system of education and you may well have been part of it as a pupil, a parent or an educator.

The links between banking education, alienation and oppression

There are two things we can be very clear about. One is that Freire's view of education was essentially political; the other is that throughout the modern world there is widespread anger and alienation in young people. Many of these young people are the products of the banking systems of education operating in their countries combined with other social and economic factors which oppress them. So this alienation can be explained as 'the separation of the subject from [an] ontological vocation of active human participation in the world' (Frymer 2005: 3). In everyday language this means that young people being educated without having a voice lose any sense of agency so that they become incapable of acting on or changing their world. What is interesting now is how many young people, largely through social networking and the easy and immediate flow of information via the Internet, are able to find others like themselves and, at the same time, a voice with which to vocalise and act out their anger. It is important to remember, however, that the effects of an education system which does not allow for questioning and dialogue has meant that generations of young people have had to put up silently with no jobs, little money, decreasing welfare services, limited access to higher education and more.

You may recall from an earlier chapter how McInerney (2009) argued that while many of the forces of domination have a long history, new modes of dehumanisation and objectification have arisen from late capitalism. In many respects, youth identity has become a commodity that is being bought by media conglomerates and sold back to the young people. Young people wear, watch, eat, drink and act in the ways in which they are being shown as being 'cool' or acceptable. This saturation of youth consciousness by the media effectively undermines active political and social engagement on the part of young people as they appear to be inclined to submit to the dominant images of society—images which are largely uninterrupted and subjected to little critical evaluation. Efforts to promote critical literacy seem especially relevant where student aspirations for the good life are often confined to gazing into shop windows for goods that lie outside their economic reach.

The argument that oppressive bad schooling contributes to alienation, especially for the most marginalised students, is powerful. We have seen in an earlier chapter how schools become complicit in this, treating young people as objects and making learning disconnected from their lives and aspirations. In his introduction to the 2001 edition of *Pedagogy of Freedom* Stanley Aronowitz, a journalist who writes widely on issues relating to modern America, argues that the banking or transmission theory of knowledge is alive and kicking in American schools where the old philosophy of liberal education has been replaced by a training model where teachers teach to externally administered tests and students engage in meaningless rote learning. This is certainly true of schools here.

It follows that in this type of education, where knowledge is the gift from the knowledgeable to the knowledge-less, there is a huge divide between teacher and learner. The teacher sees herself as in control and presents this view of herself to the students. She must, then, view the students as absolutely ignorant in order to justify her existence. The students learn to remain passive, appear ignorant, never raise questions and rarely contest what is said or offered.

Banking education maintains and fosters contradictions which may mirror features of oppressive societies. Here are some of these for you to consider.

> The teacher teaches and the students are taught.
> The teacher knows everything and the students know nothing.
> The teacher thinks and the students are thought about.
> The teacher talks and the students listen—meekly.
> The teacher disciplines and the students are disciplined.
> The teacher chooses and enforces his choice, and the students comply.
> The teacher acts and the students have the illusion of action through the action of the teacher.
> The teacher chooses the programme content, and the students (who were not consulted) adapt to it.
> The teacher confuses the authority of knowledge with his or her own professional authority which she and he sets in opposition to the freedom of the students.
> The teacher is the subject of the learning process, while the students are mere objects. (Freire 1993: 54)

(Note: I have changed the American spellings to match the content of this book.)

You will remember how important the political was in all of Freire's thinking and you can see the seeds of it here. It is his contention that this system of banking education allows those with the power to view those without as adaptable and manageable beings. After all, they have endured years of sitting passively being filled up with often meaningless information. They have not been able to develop critical consciousness which they might have been able to do had their questions been raised and addressed, their culture valued, their experience drawn on. The more completely they experienced and accepted passivity the more they adapted to and accepted the world as it is. It is very evident that banking education destroys the *creative powers* of students.

Many years ago I was fortunate enough to meet and talk with Loris Malaguzzi, the founder of the now famous preschool provision in Reggio Emilia in Italy. He emerged as a teacher at the end of the Second World War and dedicated his life to ensuring that young children would never again have to be passively educated by the nuns but should have all possible opportunities to raise questions, develop hypotheses, use every possible means to express themselves as they made sense of the physical, social, emotional and cultural worlds they inhabited. I asked him what would happen to them when they left the preschools and entered the primary/secondary school system. He replied 'Through a pedagogy of listening and interaction we enable them to work alone or collaboratively, using their hundred languages, to address what interests or scares or excites them. We think this will be a solid enough foundation to sustain them through years of passivity and tedium at school. We believe that they will emerge as full, creative, communicative, collaborative and equal citizens' (personal communication).

For Freire the role of those seeking to maintain such systems of education is to focus on trying to change the consciousness of the oppressed and not the situations that oppress them. So often these systems are supported by paternalistic social action approaches. Think about how governments talk about welfare scroungers, single mothers, homeless people, the disabled and others in terms of individual people who have somehow fallen out of the net of those who are good and organised and just. The oppressed people, says Freire, are seen as the pathology of the healthy society and they need to be integrated or incorporated into the healthy society from which they have become marginalised.

Who are the oppressed?

The very word *oppressed* carries with it images of people being subjugated, treated badly, deprived and insulted. It suggests people who are living outside of society, marginalised and alienated. But the truth is that often those who are oppressed are disadvantaged by virtue of belonging to particular groups—the very young, the very old, women, black people, the poor and so on. They may be oppressed by the exercise of power by a ruling group but also by well-intentioned liberals making decisions on their behalf. In essence what it means to oppress people is to limit or remove the potential for any individual or group to be fully human. Which of these would you describe as oppressive?

1. A system which decides where different groups of people may live (as in apartheid South Africa);
2. A system which says that only men may vote in elections (as it used to be in the UK);
3. A system which says that only those with a certain income level may go to University even if this is implied rather than baldly stated;
4. A system which insists that only children who have been inoculated against communicable diseases may go to state schools (as in Australia).

I would suggest that the first three are certainly oppressive but the fourth one is more difficult because it has been introduced in order to protect the health of all children which seems to me more than merely well-intentioned but really important to the survival of the community.

People can be oppressed in different ways. The most obvious is through being *exploited* where, for example, people's labour is used to produce profit for those in charge without the workers being adequately compensated. Sweat shops are an easy example to cite. People can be oppressed by being *marginalised* which involves being relegated to a lower social/ economic/cultural group. This is the process of exclusion and it operates on the basis of race, religion, gender, age, marital status, being unemployed or having a disability. Think about what is said about single parents, Muslims, immigrants and more.

We have seen that Karl Marx analysed alienation and was concerned at how in capitalist societies some people have power and others not. The powerless are effectively governed by those with power and one of the functions of banking education is to maintain that situation. If you educate the powerless to a very limited extent, filling them up with 'knowledge', you can control both what they learn and how they perceive themselves. You may have heard it said of Harriet Tubman, who was a runaway slave in America, who said: 'I would have freed thousands more if they had known they were slaves'. Think about this. It is so telling. It describes what Freire called a *culture of silence*. Those who are being oppressed become so powerless that they do not even talk about what is happening to them. They don't talk about the injustices, insults and acts against them. They have neither voice nor will.

How does this happen? According to Freire those in power—those who make the laws, construct the curricula, decide on the teaching methods and actually teach, systematically remind the students that they are inferior, naturally inferior, to the ruling class. They remind them that this inferiority is just part of life. If you are given the message, day after day, that you are naturally inferior you will eventually internalise this message so that it becomes part of what you believe. In this way the oppressed are dehumanised: they choose to remain silent.

You may find this extract about a Finnish boy whose family relocated to Sweden very moving. He talks of how he became marginalised simply by being different and speaking a different language. Through the educational processes he endured he lost his identity, his language, his voice and his future.

> My parents were welcome, sure enough, but as far as we kids were concerned, matters were altogether different. After all, we were not useful, productive, and on top of everything else we couldn't even speak Swedish. The principal of my new school did not really know what to do with me when I was admitted: she was just as embarrassed and at a loss as I was, and when she escorted me to the elementary third-grade classroom we walked hand in hand. Holding hands was the only language we had in common. There was a vacant seat in the rear of the classroom. The boy I was placed next to protested vehemently, but I was ordered to stay put, anyhow. The flush-faced fellow whose bench I had to share was named Osmo. It was a Finnish name and he came from Finland, but even so for some reason he refused to speak a word of Finnish. Later, I came to understand why he behaved as he did; and if I had only guessed that his fate would also be mine, I would have taken to my heels and run for my life. (Jalava in Skutnabb-Kangas and Cummins 1988: 162)

The final means of silencing people is *cultural imperialism*. We have all encountered some aspects of cultural imperialism where the culture of the ruling class becomes the norm. Those who control the society have the power to determine how people in the society communicate and interpret. What happens is that the beliefs and values, goals and achievements of the powerful become those that are valued and prized—way beyond what is possible for those not part of the ruling class. Think about modern England where there is a strong feeling that the values and beliefs and ambitions and goals of society are those determined by young men who went to Eton and now run the country. How about the cultural imperialism of Nazi Germany where the prevailing ethos was that of deciding there was a master race and finding others—Jews, homosexuals, gypsies and others—barely human.

The intersection between the work of Paulo Freire and the world of early childhood development

Jeanne Gilliam Fain (2008) carried out some research with young, largely bilingual children sharing books and stories together and talking about self-concept in relation to how language is seen and responded to. In talking about the events in stories the children identified unfairness and injustice and were particularly interested in why 'bad people behave badly'. Fain says that the children, talking openly to one another and to the adults involved, were trying out their ideas and testing their responses in a dialogic situation where they were both listeners and speakers. We know that Freire argued that dialogue is a way of knowing and is situated in wider cultural, social and political tensions within the world. He was certain that within dialogue critical thinking is essential and that within dialogue the building of identity takes place. Where you are being kept silent for one reason or another the impact on your construction of identity will be negative. Where, however, you are invited to share your thoughts, ideas, feelings and questions with others you are in a position to make connections with others and thus gain a more powerful voice.

Her project involved a year-long classroom study where twenty-two young children and their teacher talked about books. Of the twenty-two young children in the study, nineteen were Latino, one was Chinese American and two were European American students. There were thirteen girls and nine boys. The teacher used Spanish as a support in the classroom and wanted to validate the home languages and cultures of the children in the class. Much of the work took place through literature circles, sometimes family led and sometimes in school. The research question was what issues arising from the carefully chosen books did the children discuss. Freire, you may remember, said that oppression has a dehumanising effect not only on the oppressed but also on the oppressor who loses sight of those being oppressed as humans and begins to think of and treat them like objects. The children in the study were interested in why bad people (the oppressors) behave as they do, causing pain or hurt to others and seemingly not to realise what they are doing. Talking about several stories where the white people are oppressing others, one little girl, Maria, was insistent that the oppressors weren't thinking about their thinking. They didn't know how to work together.

This is, of course, a very small study and nothing much can be gleaned from it other than that when invited to talk about real issues affecting the lives of everyday people, even very young children can understand that those in power must have difficulty in recognising the effects of these actions.

Looking back, looking ahead

In this chapter we have looked at Freire's characterisation of many educational settings as following a banking model of education. You will recognise this as something of a caricature and it is important to be cautious about describing most classrooms and settings like this. In many settings where there are young learners those teaching them know about the importance of letting the children work collaboratively, to share their ideas, to explore their own interests and to be part of what one hopes is a dialogic learning situation. Sadly, the older learners become, the greater the tendency to fill them up with the facts they will need to be able to pass the exams which they will take. There are, of course, notable and significant exceptions to this. We will look at examples of these in the next chapter.

Chapter 7

Part 2: what kind of teaching and learning do we want?

In this chapter we continue to examine styles of teaching and learning and move away from the banking method to look at what Freire called the *problem-posing model, dialogic/liberatory education* or *education for critical consciousness*. In this chapter we focus largely on the role of speaking and listening in dialogic education, drawing on models drawn up by Freire and much later by Robin Alexander.

Summing up what has already been said

Freire was urging a dialogical approach to education where the teachers and learners, although not on an equal footing, can learn from one another as they investigate together the object of knowledge. You will remember that in his programmes to teach adult illiterates he devised a process where the learners were asked to stand back from something very familiar to them so that they could see it in a more critical light. This happened when the learners were shown an image of something very familiar to them and were then able to pick out what, about that image of a place or a situation or a task, interested or concerned them. The key idea was that it is the very ability to step back and think about something that allows the learner to potentially act on or change or transform it. So *thought* itself is a vital part of the process and this is the process of *praxis*, a key concept in Freire's work.

The key role of talk and thought in dialogic learning

In considering the role of spoken language in learning it is important to explore some of the ideas of Lev Vygotsky who wrote a great deal about it. In his book *Thought and Language* (first published in 1934) he explained the explicit and deep connection between speech and thought. In Freirean terms Vygotsky was examining the connections between naming and reading the world. It is only with thought that we are able to analyse and criticise and hence act on our world. Vygotsky was interested in how both silent inner speech and audible spoken language relate to thinking. In essence he believed that inner speech developed from external speech by means of becoming *internalised*, with the young child having first to think out loud by commenting to herself before being able think without the assistance of speech. Internalisation is one of Vygotsky's key concepts. Memory, like speech, later becomes internalised as thought. Memory, speech and thought are social in origin. Human infants live within families, social groups, neighbourhoods, cultures and societies. They begin to name and read their particular worlds from birth. And they do this in all the social contexts in their lives.

The intersection between the work of Paulo Freire and the world of early childhood development

Let's try and make sense of this by looking at what happens with young children. The very young child performs actions or uses words or cultural tools and signals without fully understanding their significance. An example is the young child who is always told to say 'thank you' when given something and does so without understanding the reasons why. What the child does know is that this action gets a positive response from the significant adults in her world but she doesn't really understand why saying one word or phrase is regarded as 'polite' whilst not saying it is regarded as 'rude'. When an infant, trying out the sounds of her language, repeats the sound 'ma' to produce 'mama', she is rewarded with a smile or a kiss. Children's responses are almost always responded to, often positively, which reinforces the behaviour, sometimes negatively. But this reinforcement alone cannot account for the fact that the vast majority of young children learn to speak their first language(s) within the first two years of life. Reward plays a part, as does imitation, but – as we have seen – learning a language is much more complicated than that. The first words that the human infant learns are nouns. They are the easiest to learn because they are related to objects. Verbs, referring to actions are not so evident, nor are conjunctions and as for adjectives and adverbs ...

Here we come to clear links to the work of Freire.

As children start to speak they are *naming their world*. For Vygotsky, the child's earliest *speech is already social* in the sense that it is always about communication with others. Language is essentially about communication and one of the primary ways of communicating is through *speaking and listening*. The child is naming and reading the world because everything is set in a culture and a context. Freire would have learned the names of the mango tree in his garden and of the tanager and flycatcher who built their nests nearby. Vygotsky might have learned the names of the Russian olive trees and of the arctic loon or the little grebe that flew overhead.

Vygotsky saw *egocentric speech* – which is speaking a loud to oneself (common in very young children and often in older people) – as a transition from speaking out loud to thinking. What he meant was that young children need first to say aloud what they are doing or questioning before they can think this. This vocalisation is egocentric speech. When the child no longer needs to vocalise thought, the egocentric speech has been internalised. So outer speech has become inner speech.

Here are some examples of the process human infants go through from imitating the sounds they hear, developing the muscles needed for the production of sound, engaging in making and sharing meaning using this and other means like pointing, to finally beginning to name and categorise. They are all drawn from the developmental diaries kept by the children's mothers.

- Eta chatters to herself, usually in her cot, making sounds like 'aba aba' or 'da' and 'ba'.
- Thando lies under the tree clicking. She uses her tongue and her lips. Our language (Xhosa) has click sounds in it.

Eta and Thando are both practising the sounds they have heard and developing their muscle skills in producing them. Did you know that, at birth, babies are potentially able to make the sounds of all human languages but that this ability falls away as they hear and reproduce the sounds of their own language or languages?

- Theo stares at something he wants and sometimes makes noises to accompany this. If we don't understand or respond he stares at us and then at the object he wants. It is very funny!

Theo has learned that pointing can be a tool to accomplish something. Here we see him using eye pointing where he looks intently at what he wants. He is clearly communicating a need or a desire.

- Demi looked at an orange and I responded by asking 'Do you want this orange? Is this what you want?' as I held it up. I was rewarded with a big grin and a nod of the head.

Demi, too, used eye pointing but also body language by nodding her agreement to being given an orange. So the communication is a two-way process.

Later the child may start to accompany her actions with sounds – again as a way of communicating her needs or desires. She hears the sounds of her language through all her interactions with family members and learns that sounds can operate as signs which can be used to interact with others and to satisfy needs and desires. It is now that the child starts wanting things named. This is what Nella's mum put in her diary about this:

- We took the children to the zoo and I kept pointing to the animals and saying their names. Nella, who is fifteen months old, kept saying 'cat' and pointing to each animal in turn. It seemed to us that she knew they were animals and her cat is an animal and so she called all the animals 'cat'. Three months later Nella has started going 'Wot dat?' and pointing to the object she wants named. It is constant and exhausting.

Through these little pen portraits of young children becoming communicators we see just how they are naming and reading their world through their interactions with the world and the people in it. We are also seeing how, through their interactions with those who pay close attention to them and make every effort to understand what they are needing and the silent questions they are posing, they are beginning to be able to act on the world. These are not passive empty vessels but communicating, questioning and active beings. Much of this is drawn from Smidt (2009) *Introducing Vygotsky*.

Teachers listening and talking

We have established that someone who wants to teach in a way that involves dialogue must be prepared to both relinquish the role of expert holder of knowledge and value the importance of spoken language in the classroom or setting. We know that this happens quite freely in early years settings where children are encouraged and allowed to talk as they play and learn.

Indeed in early years settings, practitioners are aware of the importance of monologues as tools in learning and good early years settings are places buzzing with noise. The same cannot be said for other classrooms in schools or colleges of adult education. Recent evidence has shown that in traditional classrooms teachers talk and students listen with the teacher asking questions where the answers relate to what has been learned already and memorised rather than to either solving or asking questions. Some recent research has also focused on the sort of talk that takes place in classrooms and if you are interested in this you can read the work of Alexander (2006) or Mercer and Littleton (2007).

Here are some case studies and as you read them decide how dialogic the questions asked by the teacher are. The first one is one of my favourite pieces of writing. It comes from Vivan Gussin Paley's wonderful book called *Wally's Stories*. Paley, working with very young children, began to listen carefully to them and through this changed her style of teaching, using narrative and theatre in the classroom. Here is a bit about God and bad thoughts.

Teacher: *Where do you children get all these ideas about wishing?*
Andy: From God. He makes up everything.
Wally: First God thinks it up to Himself and then He puts it into your mind.
Eddie: But some ideas come from your mother and father.
Wally: After God puts it into their mind.
Deana: I think it just comes from your mind. Your mind tells you what to think.
Eddie: Here's how it happens. You remember things other people say and you see everything, and then your mind gives you spaces to keep all the rememberings and then you say it.
Wally: Don't forget, Eddie, that God makes you remember. He tells you if it's a good idea.
Lisa: Maybe it's a bad idea.
Wally: He tells bad people bad things.
Teacher: *Why is that?*
Wally: So the good people can tell the bad people to be good.

(Paley 1981: 34–5)

The teacher asks only two questions, each relating to what the children have been talking about. Neither of these questions sets out to test the children. All the questions do is show the children that the teacher is not only listening to them but interested in what they are saying. She is treating them as serious learners.

And here is another example, this time taken from the terrible real-life incident of the Zeebrugge ferry which some six- and seven-year-old children saw on television the night before and wanted to talk about. After being drawn into the children's talk the teacher gave them paper and drawing materials, thinking this would help them deal with their questions and their fears. She then listened to what they were saying and took notes.

Two of the children had been on ferries to France and both drew detailed pictures of people in the bar as the water starting pouring in. One of these children, Alex, accompanied his drawing with a running commentary:

> When we went to France we had croissants for breakfast. That's what you have when you go to France . . . These are the trays of salad and they are going to fall off . . . SPLAT! . . . into the water. All the plates and cups and knives and things are just smashing off the tables and here's the water starting to come in . . . This man here, this one, he's just falling against the wall and it hurts . . . OW . . . Here's the man, the one, you know, he made himself a bridge so that people could get out. My dad said if it happened to us, first we would save the baby, then me, then my mum and then my dad.

At this point he was interrupted by a very distressed Fiona, saying

> 'No! If that ever happens to us my mum PROMISES she'll be saved first. I wouldn't want to be alive without my mum'.

Both the children have given the people in their pictures speech bubbles saying not only words like 'Help!' or 'Oh, no!' but things that are deeply moving as where Fiona has a man and his son in the water with the man saying 'Swim to me, son' and the boy replying 'OK'. In the opposite corner of the picture a little girl cries out 'Where's mum?' Alex has drawn the man stretched over the tables so that his body makes a bridge for people to walk across. Standing next to him is a little boy saying 'You can do it, dad!'

A third child had been very affected by the disaster which she had watched at home and talked about with her family. She could not believe that water could be heavy enough to capsize such a large vessel. All the children believed that it was because all the vehicles on the ferry – the cars and lorries – had slipped to one side. This is what she wrote:

THE FERRY TIPPED OVER BECOS THEY LEFT THE DOORS OPEN. MOST PEOPLE SAVIVED BUT LOTS DIED PEOPLE SAY IT TOOK NO MORE THAN 10 SECONDS I'M GLAD I WASNT ON THE BOAT.

The teacher here, like Paley, was more than willing to listen to the children: both adults were genuinely interested in what the children were saying. Both of these teachers are clearly doing what Freire said in an interview with Ira Shor in 1987: *they are adopting the stance of a liberating teacher in a dialogical class.*

The characteristics of a liberating teacher

According to Freire a dialogic teacher does the following things:

- Modulates her tone of voice to ensure that it is conversational rather than didactic or overly teacherly.
- Listens carefully and with genuine interest when students are speaking and invites all those in the group to do the same thing.
- Sets up a culture where students are accustomed to not only answer questions but be willing and able to say more on the subject.
- Often starts a class by addressing some of the questions raised or issues touched on towards the end of the last class. This is a way of showing the students that the teacher has been interested in what they were saying and is willing to follow up on it. In this way the teacher is signalling that what students say matters.
- Uses a range of strategies, one of which is humour.

What do you think of this as a list of the strategies and stance that someone wanting to stimulate dialogic talk in a classroom might adopt? Remember that by stimulating dialogic talk we are looking for someone who is genuinely interested in the ideas and thoughts of the students. Let's look at what Robin Alexander wrote in 2006. He had obviously read Freire's work and been influenced by it but he was writing about a different culture and at a different time. Here are what he called his *talk descriptors* which indicate that what is taking place is dialogic.

- Teachers and children address the learning tasks together, whether as a group or as a class, rather than in isolation. So the talk descriptor for this is that the approach is *collective.*
- Teachers and children listen to each other, share ideas and consider alternatives. This approach is *reciprocal.*
- Children talk freely without fear or embarrassment about getting it wrong and they help one another to reach common understandings. This approach is *supportive.*
- Teachers and children build on their own and one another's ideas and chain them in coherent lines of thinking and enquiry. This approach is *cumulative.*

- And finally, teachers plan and facilitate dialogic teaching with particular educational goals in mind. (Alexander 2006: 28)

So the teaching is said to be *purposeful*.

Much has been written about the role of speaking and listening in education and you can read more about it if this interests you. For our purposes we are thinking about how talk can characterise the nature of teaching and illustrate powerfully what the intentions of the teachers are. In the example cited earlier of Paley and her class of young children, how would you describe her intentions? Why does she ask the questions she does or make the comments she makes?

The intersection between the work of Paulo Freire and the world of early childhood development.

Case study 1: becoming a dialogic teacher

In her book *Bad Guys Don't Have Birthdays* (1929) Paley described what happened to her that made her into a supreme example of a truly dialogic teacher. Here is what she said:

> When I was twenty, I led a Great Books discussion group in the New Orleans Public Library. The participants were older and wiser, but my lists of questions made me brave. Get the people talking, I was told, and connect their ideas to the books: there are no right or wrong answers.
>
> The procedure seemed simple enough. I moved from question to question and quite often it sounded as if it was a real discussion. Yet most of the time I was pretending. The people and the books were shadowy presences whose connections to one another seemed more real than their connections to me. What I wanted, desperately, was to avoid awkward silences. (Paley 1929: 7)

Paley became a kindergarten/nursery teacher soon afterwards and to do the job, she was equipped with curriculum guides and still believed it was her job to fill the time in with few distractions, looking for as many correct answers as possible. She said that it never occurred to her that the distractions might have been the sounds of the children thinking. Remember this! It is a wonderful way of thinking. After some time a visiting science teacher of older children asked if he could spend time in the kindergarten. He had a new grandchild who was due to start in a nursery and wanted to have a go at teaching very young children himself. So Bill arrived equipped with his 'paper bags full of show and tell' (ibid.: 7) and she noticed how much the children talked and listened and how much the teacher talked and listened and built on what the children said. Paley watched and listened herself and worked out what she saw to be the recipe: ask a question or make a casual observation, then repeat each comment given in response and hang onto it until a link can be made to a previous statement. In Paley's words 'He and the children were constructing paper chains of ideas, factual and magical and Bill supplied the glue' (ibid.: 7).

This notion of paper chains of ideas is one that really interests me and you will find examples of it throughout this book. It perfectly illustrates Alexander's talk descriptor of *cumulative*.

Case study 2: using questions in the classroom

Neil Mercer and his colleagues think a great deal about dialogue as an educational tool and have written widely about it. In their work they remind us of some things we will know to be true. In many teaching situations the talk of the teacher dominates and much of the talk is in the form of questions. Often the questions are those that can be called initiation-response feedback or IRF exchanges. These questions are specifically designed to check whether the learner has understood what is required or is on the same wavelength as the teacher. Here are two of just such questions and the responses from the children.

- The teacher asks 'So what are our talk rules?' to which one reply is 'When someone else is talking you don't call out'.
- The teacher asks 'When do you come into contact with the soil?' to which the child replies 'under trees, near around the trees and around bushes and everything'.

You can see that the function of these questions is to check on how well the children are following or engaged in the discussion or activity. Mercer reminds us that questions can serve different communicative functions. They can be used to find out what the learners know and understand; to manage classroom activities and also to find out more about what the pupils are doing and thinking.

Robin Alexander says that if we look beneath the seeming similarity of talk in classrooms the world over we will find that teachers organise talk in classrooms in very different ways. In most of the classrooms he observed he noted that teachers talk more than the pupils; but the balance and the nature of contributions varies considerably, according to the nature of the classroom, where it is situated and what the prevailing culture and ethos is. One of the reasons for this variation seems to be that in some classrooms a teacher's questions (or other prompts) might elicit only brief responses from pupils, while in others they often generate much more extended and reflective talk. Alexander contends that what he calls *dialogic talk* describes a particularly effective type of classroom interaction. 'Dialogic talk' is where both teachers and pupils make substantial and significant contributions towards something of interest or concern to the learner and which then helps the learners' thinking to move forward.

Here, to illustrate this is Mercer's example which was recorded in an English primary school by Open University researcher Manuel Fernandez, who is investigating the role of computers in children's literacy development. In this extract, the teacher is talking with some members of her year 5/6 class about their current activity; they are communicating by e-mail with members of a class in another local school about the shared curriculum topic 'How to have a healthy lifestyle'. The teacher's words are in italics.

Teacher:	*Right. Somebody is going to read this to me now.*
Declan:	'Dear Springdale. In science we are looking at the healthy human body. We need a lot of exercise to keep our muscles, hearts and lungs working'.
Samia:	'Working well'.
Declan:	'Working well. It also keeps our bones strong'.
Samia:	Yeah. We don't need a full stop.
Teacher:	*Yeah. That's fine. That's all right. Carry on. 'Flies . . . '*
Declan:	'Flies and other animals can spread diseases and germs. That is why it is very important to keep food stored in clean cupboards, etcetera'.
Evan:	Is cupboards spelled wrong? (It is written 'cubourds')
Teacher:	*Yes, it is spelled wrong actually. It is cup-boards. Cup-boards.*
Samia:	(Reading as teacher writes) B-O-A-R-D-S.
Teacher:	*It's a difficult word.*
Evan:	O, A.
Teacher:	*OK. Can I ask you a question? And etcetera is ETC, not ECT. I want to ask you a question before you carry on. So why have you felt it is important as a group to send Springdale this information?*
	(Several children speak together)

Teacher:	*Just a minute. Let's have one answer at a time.*
Samia:	Cause if they haven't done it yet. We can give them the information . . .
Teacher:	*Yeah.*
Samia:	. . . that we have found in the book and so when they do get – when they do this part they will know, they will know, so, to answer it.
Teacher:	*OK. Excellent. So what were you going to say Declan?*
Declan:	So they can have a healthy body and they can use it for information.
Teacher:	*OK.*
Evan:	And plus, if they haven't got the books.
Teacher:	*And if they haven't got the books. Now before you tell me anything else you've found in a book, I think, don't know what you think, do you think it would be a good idea to tell them why you are . . . what you've just explained to me? We are sending you this information because . . .*
Samia:	'Just because, we couldn't find, something like . . . '
Declan:	'They could be doing it right now'.
Teacher:	*Well, they might be.*
Samia:	'We are sending you this piece of information just in case you haven't done it yet, to help you'.
Teacher:	*Right, discuss it how you want to say that. OK?*

(http://orbit.educ.cam.ac.uk/wiki/The_educational_
value_of_dialogic_talk_in_whole-class_dialogue)

Reading that again enabled me to get the sense of just how like a normal dialogue or discussion it was. It could have been taking place anywhere. It did not feel stilted or closed like so many classroom discussions I come across in my reading. Mercer's (2003) analysis of this is interesting. He sees that much of the teacher's questioning serves to help the children reflect on and consider their own thinking. The teacher in this example often picks on and repeats a child's response and this enables the child to share her responses with others – a step towards thinking and problem solving collaboratively. In all of this the teacher is assisting the children in using language as a tool for thought. Mercer believes that through helping teachers learn to think carefully about how one might use questions constructively in teaching and learning situations, they begin to be able to encourage children to engage in both solitary and collective thinking: a goal close to Paulo Freire's heart. To use his language: they are becoming better able to read and write their worlds.

Looking back, looking ahead

In this, the second of two chapters looking at what kind of teaching and learning we might want, we have spent much time examining the use of talk and dialogue in learning situations. This is an enormous area and one open to much debate. Some will feel strongly that having a dialogic approach to learning is essential to enable learners to take control of aspects of their own lives. For them education is essentially about being able to criticise and vocalise thoughts about what is right and what is wrong with their worlds. Learners able to do this have the possibility of changing aspects of their lives. Others may feel that what matters most for learners is the end result – the exam they will pass, the qualification they will get, the ranking they will attain. In the next chapter we continue looking at teaching and learning, this time turning our attention to the book Freire wrote with Ira Shor in 1987.

Chapter 8

A pedagogy for liberation

In this chapter we spend more time on examining aspects of the dialogical model of teaching and we do this through examining what the authors call a dialogic presentation about dialogic pedagogy – in an interactive work in which Ira Shor and Paulo Freire (1986) discuss aspects of dialogic or liberatory education. The book is called *A Pedagogy for Liberation*. The chapter will be presented in the form of some of the questions Shor asks Freire followed by the answers Freire gives. I am paraphrasing both questions and answers, only occasionally using direct quotations. Shor's questions are in bold text.

Shor: **Do you believe that the teacher is both an artist and a politician, as you have stated? It seems that the politics of the dialogical pedagogy are clearer than its aesthetics. Can you start by analysing the process of dialogue and then working through to the aesthetics of the method?**

Freire: First of all we must be clear about what we mean when we talk of dialogue. It is not a technique which we can use to get certain results and it is also not a tactic we can use to become friends with our students. That would make dialogue a technique for manipulation rather than illumination. Dialogue has come about as the result of more and more people becoming both communicative and critical – of becoming able to read their worlds. As human beings we not only know what we know but also what we don't know. It is this knowledge that enables us, through dialogue, to transform reality. It is important to remember that we communicate in social settings: communication is always social. Dialogue arises out of our history as human beings. *Dialogue is a moment where humans meet to reflect on their reality as they make and remake it* (1982: 13).

Shor: **Would you agree that communication is not just an exchange of words but also affirms or challenges the relationships between those** communicating, what they are talking about and where all this takes place?

Freire: Dialogue is a challenge to existing domination. One of the most important features of dialogue is that what is being discussed does not belong solely to one person but is a shared concern of the whole group. The teacher is not the one who holds the knowledge about what is being discussed and graciously passes this on to the students. The subject is mediated between the teacher and the learners. It is up for discussion not a given. There will be multiple questions to ask, views to consider and possibly many answers. It is true that the teacher may have chosen the topic for discussion but must still allow for the views of others to be heard and respected. We might say that the teacher may know more about the subject at the start of a lesson but has to relearn what she knows after discussion with the students. *Dialogue is the sealing together of the teachers and the students in the joint act of knowing and re-knowing the object of study. Then, instead of transferring the knowledge statically, as a fixed possession of the teacher, dialogue demands a dynamic approximation towards the object* (ibid: 14).

Shor: **Would you accept that some educators in the First World find this notion of the 'teacher as learner' bizarre?**

Freire: Certainly. Many people say that the idea which comes from the Third World is beautiful but not applicable to the First World where it is accepted that the role of the teacher is to teach. Of course all teachers have the role to teach but for me this involves accepting that I, as a teacher, don't hold the knowledge and that my students, whose interests and lives fascinate me, have much to teach me about what I already know and about things I know nothing of. *Then both of us can illuminate the object together* (ibid: 15).

Shor: **The formal lecture situation sets up the teacher as authority who transfers fixed knowledge to students and does this verbally. In contrast the openness of the dialogic teacher offers up a more democratic and equal approach. Would you agree that if the dialogical teacher announces that he or she is relearning material through dialogue this challenges his or her position. The challenges offered by the views and voices of students may demystify the teacher's power.**

Freire: It is true but it is important to say that no teacher relearns everything through dialogue. What happens is that teachers have to demonstrate their *competency* to the students and this competency involves having time to know the students and their concerns, time to listen to them and respect what they are interested in. We need to remember that dialogue is always context-bound. Part of the context is the political context. Dialogue cannot take place in some sort of free space where anything goes. *To achieve the goals of transformation, dialogue implies responsibility, directiveness, determination, discipline, objectives* (ibid: 16). Remember that the presence of dialogue implies the absence of *authoritarianism* and it is important to note that dialogue does not require everyone to speak.

Shor: I understand that you are saying that it would be wrong for individuals to feel pressured to speak. This would create a fake situation where dialogue becomes just a dogma. But I must ask if you think that the right to stay silent means the right to sabotage the process? In my experience I have seen classes where so many have remained silent that the whole dialogic process has been hijacked. Do you think that situated learning might offer a good route into increasing student participation?

Freire: The training and experience of teachers often makes them distant from reality. The very concepts that are studied are remote from the realities of most people's lives. We become experts in this game of concepts and then our language risks losing contact with concreteness. And in this way we move further and further from the masses of people. I do insist on dialogical education starting from the students' understanding of their daily life experiences. The students can be at college or university, in preschool or primary school. They may be kids or workers, young or old. But in every case it is their description of their daily lives which offers the possibility of reaching a rigorous understanding of reality. I agree with Gramsci that scientific rigor comes from an effort to overcome a naive understanding of the world. *Science is superimposing critical thought on what we observe in reality, after the starting point of common sense . . . If I am no longer naive, it means that I am no longer acritical* (ibid: 19–20). This is the first transition to critical consciousness.

Interlude: the story of 'From Astrology to Astronomy'

In the midst of the discussion Freire launched into a story which I am going to retell here. It is about a friend of his from Brazil, a physics professor who taught a course called 'From Astrology to Astronomy' which he described as being a history of what rigor in science means. He explained that he asked the physics students at the very start of the course to go into an area where common people live and ask them about their worlds – worlds which include the sky, the stars, the planets, the sun and moon. They questioned workers, peasants, fishermen, or people in the street. How did they see their world and understand it? What did they know about the cosmos and what did the stars mean to them? How far away did they think the stars were? He invited the students to write their answers to these question.

What he was seeking to do was to research *popular thinking* about reality. When the physics students came into class they reported on the things the ordinary people had said about the sun and moon, day and night, the seasons, tides coming in and going out and compared all these to their own responses. The assumption he made was that the students' own positions would be less magical than those of the people they had questioned. And, as you will have guessed, they were.

Then he began to think and work scientifically with them on this material. He told Freire that many of his colleagues and critics worried about this approach because it was moving away from the traditional, the required, the assessed curriculum. He went on to say that he was not opposed to the curriculum per se but opposed to the often elitist and authoritarian way of organising studies and learning. The professor had set up *situated research* (which meant carrying out the research in the context of everyday life) and used that as the starting point for moving on, working collaboratively and making serious contact with ordinary people, using mass culture as a research tool. The students became active researchers before having had a single lecture.

My turn to ask you, the reader, a question. **Do you think the students have been empowered through this approach?**

In fact this was the very question Shor asked of Freire after he had heard the story. Here is how Freire responded:

> The word 'empowerment,' so popular in the United States causes me great concern. I fear that the feeling is that once students have 'been empowered' the story is over. The work of the educator is finished. The teacher is no more than a lamp-lighter. The truth is that even if the students in the physics course had been empowered they were still very far from being autonomous enough to transform society. Individual empowerment is fine, but transformation of any society depends on all students being empowered. The critical development of students is essential but not sufficient to guarantee societal change.

Shor: You began your work in Brazil. I live in the United States where we have a deep devotion to individuals making their own way, pulling ourselves up by our proverbial bootstraps and all that. It is a culture in love with the self-made man. Our history is dark. We kept slaves, massacred Native Americans in huge numbers and we place the emphasis on self in education as everywhere else. Is it possible to use your approach which was developed in the Third World?

Freire: In order to answer this I have to talk about social class empowerment rather than individual or community or social empowerment. This may very well scare the people of the USA. We are accustomed to thinking about class in Brazil but it is a concept that is hard to apply to the complex societies of the US. I am not a strict Marxist in my thinking about social class empowerment but what I think needs to be considered is how the working class or classes can be introduced to using their own experience, their own construction of culture in order to access political power. Empowerment here becomes a political process by the dominated classes who seek their own freedom from this domination. In short it is a long historical process where education is just one front. Another point I want to make about the culture of the USA is the overwhelming predominance of self-help books which stimulate individuality and not collaboration. Another thing that fascinates me about the USA is how myth and reality co-exist side by side as do evil and good, devil and angel. This is an extremely difficult culture to learn.

Shor: I want to ask you again the question of the teacher as artist. Can we call teachers artists? As a teacher myself I try and be creative, just as your friend the physics professor was and I know that the creative disruption of passive education is both an aesthetic moment and a political one because it requires students to examine their prior understandings and to practice new ways as learners together with the teacher. I try to modulate my voice as a teacher so that I use a conversation pattern rather than a stern lecturing tone. I listen to the students and ask other students to listen too. I don't begin my response to a student when he or she says something but ask the student to elaborate. And I use humour and love it when my students do the same, often mimicking me or other teachers. They often do this with consummate skill.

Freire: As educators we all have a role to play in the process of formation or growing up, which means a role to play in our students growing up. I see this process as an artistic one. Growing up means being shaped and must involve some aesthetic moments. More than that education is an act of knowing and for me knowing is beautiful. *To the extent that knowing is unveiling an object, the unveiling gives the object 'life', calls it into 'life', even gives it a new 'life'. This is an artistic task because our knowing has a life-giving quality, creating and animating objects as we study them* (ibid: 31). If education takes place informally – at home for instance – or formally, those involved with the growing learner are doing the artistic or aesthetic task of helping to form the person they will become. This is a creative process in itself.

The intersection between the work of Paulo Freire and the world of early childhood development

This is the true story of a piece of situated learning which took place in the Italian city of Reggio Emilia a few years ago. As you read it look out for some of the things you have just read about the ideas of Ira Shor and Paulo Freire on dialogic or liberatory education.

Elio Canova, the president of I Teatri Consortium in Reggio Emilia, had a brain wave. One of two of the curtains in the theatre was damaged and needed to be repaired and restored. Canova, a passionate supporter of the work of Reggio Children, had the inspired idea of asking the children at the preschool *Scuola Diana* to design a curtain. He knew that this was something real, relevant and culturally significant. The children knew the theatre, went there with their families and others and here was a magnificent opportunity for them to produce something real, beautiful, useful and visible for their own community.

(Note: in this section I highlight what the teachers do using a different font. This is to make it easier for you, as you read, to ask if and how the teacher is using an approach that is essentially dialogic.)

The story begins: first steps, first marks, first ideas

Those planning the project realised that it had to start as many of the projects do with a hands-on experience, in this case with a visit to the theatre. It was clear that the project would involve some issues including a recognition that the techniques used had to be economical and simple in light of the limited budget; the curtain would have to conform to safety requirements and be fire retardant; the actual enormous size of the curtain meant that it would not be possible for the children to work on the final version and decisions would have to be made about where to work, who could be involved and whether some children would have to be selected for the final stages.

The first step then was a visit to the theatre, which was a place not unfamiliar to them, but in this case they were going to be really looking at it with fresh eyes. The building itself is impressive with statues along the front, a portico below the statues, arches, windows of different shapes and sizes, reliefs and plaques on the walls and gardens.

The children walked and looked and talked and the teachers, alongside them, wrote down what they said. Here are some of the things the children said:

It's really big! It has lots of columns and a whole lot of windows.

I don't know who lives there.

They put statues on the roof so the theatre would become more important.

Maybe the statues are of the dead people who built it.

The children explored the space, running through the portico, climbing on the steps, running in and out of the columns, stroking the columns in a made-up repeated game in which they went in and out, round and round, up and down.

Then the teachers asked the children to draw the building from the outside. Then the children were taken inside where there are tiers with columns, gold everywhere, a wonderful domed and painted ceiling and more. Here is what some of the children said:

Wow! It looks like the theatre of heaven.

Look at that chandelier! It's a light with white diamonds inside it!

There's a round thing like a world that has people painted on it who are flying and horses with wings, then there are some woods, some lakes and the sky with clouds.

Then there's a thousand lights – yellow, green and red and when the show starts they go off and everything gets dark.

The teachers noted that the children became more still and talked less, as they gazed upwards in wonderment. Teachers invited the children to follow the semicircular perimeter of the stalls, running their fingers along the wall as they did so. They noted these very young children were making comparisons and using metaphor and simile when they talked about what they could see.

It's made like an arch.

It's like half an egg.

At this point the children knew nothing about the proposal for them to design the curtain for this theatre. For them it was just one of the lovely excursions they regularly enjoy. But when the children started to look at the existing curtain and talk about what it represented the teachers asked them what they would think if they were asked to design a new curtain. Here are some of their responses:

> I don't think we could do it because it would take too long, at least eleven days.
> Look, something that big can hold the ideas of all the kids. Not just one idea but lots of ideas.
> I guess somebody better go up on the stage and measure it.

The children decided to measure the width of the curtain using their bodies. Then they did it again, this time counting the number of footsteps and the number of times their open arms were used. The teachers noted that some anxiety about the size was creeping into the children's thoughts so they decided to tell the children at this point that what they will be doing is make the design smaller than the final curtain and then use special techniques to enlarge it.

How well do you think the teachers are doing up to this point in time in terms of being dialogic in their approach? Do the responses of the children give you any indication that they are being invited to ask questions and be partners in this project?

The first thing the teachers did on the return to the school was to take the children into the largest open space in the school, the piazza, and ask them to estimate and 'draw' the width of the curtain using whatever movements or measures they could find. You will remember how interested in size the children were. The children again paced out or used wide open-arm counts and then a meter stick. Although the children would initially be working on a smaller scale, some notional idea of the approximate dimensions needed to be referred back to. The teachers then asked the children for their thoughts on the theatre and the visit. They asked too why the children of this particular school had been chosen. Here are some things the children said:

> Maybe they asked us to make a new curtain because they think we're really good at it.
> I think it's because our school is the closest to the theatre.

As always the teachers listened respectfully to what the children were say-ing and noticed that one of the things that impressed most children were the elaborately patterned pieces of highly gilded stucco work all over the walls and ceiling. The children called these 'rubber stamps', perhaps in reference to rubber stamps that many had at home. They immediately set out to make their own designs for rubber stamps. In the theatre the stucco disks took many forms – flowers and leaves and ducks and birds and tendrils. The children's designs included all of these but also hearts and snakes and a wide range of patterns. There were lines and zigzags and dots and spirals. A world of line and colour.

Over the next few days all the children, in small groups, visited the theatre. Some of them visited the nonpublic areas so they could see the mechanical device for lowering the curtain or the large electrical board covered in cables and switches and some of the children made elaborate drawings, like diagrams, of these devices.

When the teachers asked what would be suitable images to put on a theatre curtain the children did not hesitate. They wanted beautiful things, things to make people feel happy, things that would be fun to draw, things that would create a feeling of peace. They insisted that scorpions or snakes or beetles could not be included but other little creatures like dragonflies and pretty grasshoppers could. The teachers concluded that the children were thinking about representing the things they liked, made them happy and were important and interesting. But they also remembered and made a note of the fact that the children had been very interested earlier in the year in insects in the springtime and felt that some of this was influenc-ing their choices.

So the drawing began. The children could use a range of resources for this. These children had all had much experience in this area and were used to having the support of the *atelierista* (an artist in residence in a studio on the premises). They could draw their plants or creatures or the sun from real observation, through exploring images in books, through memory or invention. Keen that the children should retain a sense of the things they were drawing being alive, the teachers tried to embed in the process some discussion and investigation of scientific processes relating to how plants grow, what energy is and so on: they call this the pulsing of life.

Here we have the teacher as expert intervening to tell or remind children of things that they might not already know. Does the teacher moving into the role of holder of certain knowledge fail to be dialogic by doing this?

As the children began to draw they talked and began to create narratives and look at what the other children were doing. A wonderful moment – and one that changed the whole project – was when Giovanni said 'My plant is transforming, it's in a phase of transformation' and, after a while, went on 'Why don't we do it so that the things we draw get transformed into other things?'

Vea Vecchi, the key staff member in this project, calls moments like this in the life of the *scuole dell'infanzia*, *generative moments*, where one thing steers the work in a particular direction. I guess we might call it a lightbulb moment. Freire would certainly have responded to the term 'generative moments'. But Vecchi's analysis of where Giovanni's idea came from is fascinating. She says that the children themselves are growing, and growing means change and transformation. As children they also watch a lot on television and in films where magical transformations are common and through these media very visible. They then play out transformations in school, at home, in the piazza and parks. For Vecchi transformations and metamorphosis are processes somewhere between biology (natural physical growth and change) and magic (fantastical change).

One of the teachers, Paola, started asking the children what they thought of Giovanni's idea. Do you see this as a clear invitation to the children to become equal partners in the project? The children were articulate and thoughtful in their responses. All liked the idea of transformations but they all agreed that the subject – the thing to be transformed – had to be the one to decide whether to be transformed or not. They also agreed that the subject should be allowed to return to its original state. Here the learners are clearly making decisions for themselves and being allowed to do so.

Here the teachers really showed how respectful they are of children's ownership of the processes of drawing and making. Since the subject has the right to be changed into something else and back again, each child needed access to two sheets of paper – one for the unchanged subject and one for the transformation. Should the subject want to go back to its original state, there it is, on the first sheet of paper.

The children had access to soft pencils, coloured pencils, black markers and coloured markers with thin or thick tips. They had a choice of A4 or A3 paper as well as large sheets of patterned paper. They also had access to erasers, which they love. The erasers are liberating in that they allow the child to erase mistakes easily and to successfully change the original. It is the teacher who offers all these resources in response to the observed needs of the children.

The transformations begin. Some children find it easier than others. Some seem to make unrelated doodles beside their original drawing, whilst others clearly change or transform some aspect of the original. As the children draw they offer monologues and narratives.

Giovanni drew a wonderful grasshopper and his transformation was to lengthen the grasshopper's legs. He said 'When the grasshopper is transformed he always has a little bit of leg ...'

Giorgio drew the sun and a leaf and said 'When I made the transformation of the sun, I was thinking about its energy and I made the shapes of energy. But when I made the plant I was thinking about its energy that makes it grow with its roots, with water and light'.

After time spent making lots of drawings the children were asked to select the ones they would like to see become part of the curtain. Once they had chosen these needed to be made into one composition, and this, as you can imagine, was a tricky part of the process. The teachers decided that there were two alternatives for the children:

- The tried and tested process of cutting out the chosen drawings and deciding, by trial and error, where to place them in order to make the composition.
- Use computers to scan in the drawings so they could be viewed and manipulated on the screen.

The teachers, aware of the existing and potential role of the digital revolution in the lives of coming generations, decided that the children needed to become familiar with what was possible using computers. They offered the children two programmes to use and the children, not surprisingly, learned very quickly how to use them. What the teachers wanted to do was to observe carefully what the children did as they played with the programmes on the computers. They were looking to see what methods the children used. Staff in the preschools use this process of observation and documentation as a basic, fundamental and very important part of their pedagogy. They were observing both individual and group strategies and keeping detailed notes on what they were doing.

The children, using the computer, stressed the images – in other words they used the computer to take the image to its limits by enlarging or shrinking it and noticing what happened. Here are some of their comments:

It is getting skinnier and skinnier, it disappeared!
Look at this grasshopper. It's a monster!

At this stage the children were not very interested in making multiple images, although they moved on to this later in the process. The teachers notice and comment on the fact that children, at the computers, work in silence, which is unusual for Reggio. But they do respond to what they notice by pulling faces and making exclamations of horror or glee. They also notice that the children using the computer are happy for images to overlap, whereas those using paper avoid this.

As the children's physical prowess on the computers improve, they begin to make up narratives about what they are doing. Some children work using paper, cutting and sticking to make a variety of compositions. Some children use a digital camera. Some move from computer to paper to digital camera and back again. All of this is evidence of children using new and known languages as part of their expressive vocabulary. And the teachers, observing and documenting all the time, develop and extend their languages in response.

At this point the teachers decided to ask the children to evaluate the different techniques they had been using. Here is what some of them said:

The computer is stronger: you can make them bigger or smaller and you can make them appear and then appear again; you can change it and make the designs you want.
I didn't discover anything with the computer. With the sheets of paper I moved the drawings around, one at the bottom, one at the top, one here, one there.

The final stages of making the curtain involved a number of activities and decisions. The children got involved in the process of enlarging their images onto sheets of acetate using an overhead projector. By now a smaller number of children were involved in the work and these consisted of two groups each of three children, and they became a boys' group and a girls' group. The children were selected on the basis of having been very interested in the project, the strategies they demonstrated and their competencies. The teachers were keen that there should be a real mix of strategies and competencies in each group.

The children had to reach agreement about which of the two final images should be selected to become the curtain. Not surprisingly each group argued for its own image and it is only the generosity and honesty of one of the girls, after a very lively discussion, that allowed the final decision to be made. The image made by the boys was deemed to be the better one. The last stage involved the six children going to paint the real pattern onto a plastic sheet. There was no space to do this in the school and the theatre offered the group the use of its painter's loft. Two to three children and their teachers spent twenty days in the loft working on the design. When the children had completed their work, the design was digitised and printed onto the fabric.

As the children worked painting on the acetate sheet placed on top of the enlarged black-and-white design they had agreed on, they continued to talk and look and move around. The teachers set out a wide range of paint colours and brushes and they placed a stepladder in the loft so that the children could look down on their work. The teachers suggested they do this every so often. Sometimes the children worked close together, enjoying the intimacy and opportunity to chat. Sometimes they called one another over for an opinion, advice or physical help. As they gained confidence their brush strokes became bolder and more purposeful.

Then something amazing happened. The painting was almost finished when Leonardo asked 'Why don't we put in some cells that come from outer space. And then they can decide what shape they want to be'. There was a lot of discussion about what a cell looks like and one child suggested looking in a book, another said he did not want to do that because he had a picture of cells in his mind. At this point a little girl called Mimi got up and started moving around in a spontaneous dance whilst the others drew their ideas of cells. Then she sat down and Giovanni got up to dance and this is what he said: 'I'm dancing Mimi's cell ... look, I'm following her drawing with my body ... I'm copying it by dancing. I'm copying her drawing with a dance, and before she was dancing my cell' (based on chapter 7 in Smidt 2013, *Introducing Malaguzzi*).

Looking back, looking ahead

In this chapter we have looked at a dialogue between Paulo Freire and the American educator Ira Shor, discussing what is really meant by dialogic and liberatory pedagogy. To make the link with early childhood education we examined the true story of how a group of very young children became engaged in designing a curtain for the theatre of their town. In the next chapter we turn to the work of Augusto Boal who used theatre to challenge the status quo.

Chapter 9

Theater of the Oppressed

An elaboration of the work of Paulo Freire

In this chapter we look at the work of another Brazilian, Augusto Boal. Born in 1931 in Rio de Janeiro, he was the son of a Portuguese baker, José Augustino Mario Charles Boal, and his Brazilian wife, Albertina Chantele Pinto. Augusto developed an interest in the theatre at an early age but before becoming professionally involved he studied chemical engineering, eventually to the master's level. After graduating with a first degree he went to New York in 1952 and there enrolled at the School of Dramatic Arts at Columbia University, whilst studying for his master's degree at the same time. One of his teachers at Columbia was John Gassner, who had previously taught such significant figures as Tennessee Williams and Arthur Miller. Here Boal was introduced to the theatrical and revolutionary techniques of Bertolt Brecht and Constantin Stanislavski. In 1956, shortly after graduating, he was invited to work with the Arena Theatre in São Paulo, southeast Brazil. It was during this period that he began to adapt the methods of such political directors as Brecht and Stanislavski to the conditions in Brazil. This involved him in taking a public stand against the endemic dominance of the rich over the poor, criticising the appalling living conditions of the majority of the people and, significantly, the voicelessness of the oppressed. This was, for him, a productive, appreciated but risky time in his professional and creative life.

After the new military coup in 1964 he escaped into exile in Argentina. He had first met Freire when he, Boal, was touring with Arena in the northeast province where Freire had been born. Freire, much older than Boal, exerted a powerful influence over him since they shared a keen political sensibility and awareness of the existence and effects of injustice, discrimination, poverty and alienation. When Freire died, Boal said, 'With Paulo Freire's death I lost my last father' – a truly moving tribute from one fighter for justice to another.

Note: The title of Boal's book uses the American spelling of theatre. I respect this when using the title of the book but elsewhere revert to UK spelling.

He first read *Pedagogy of the Oppressed* whilst in Argentina and the book spoke so directly to him that he began to develop a theatrical method based on Freire's ideas about liberatory education. His own analysis had already led him to see that theatre could be a powerful weapon in the hands of either the oppressors or the oppressed. Existing theatre, at the time, was often well intentioned, with the directors choosing to produce plays about important social issues, which were presented by professional actors to a passive audience of viewers. He drew parallels between what the theatre was doing and what was happening under banking education in schools, colleges and universities. He began to rethink everything, particularly how the oppressed might be liberated and whether only the oppressed themselves could achieve this. In 1979 his own book (clearly a tribute to Freire) *Teatro del Oprimido* was published and later translated into English as *Theater of the Oppressed*.

The development and impact of ALFIN (Integral Literacy Operation or *Operacion Alfabetizacion Integral*) programme

In 1973 Boal left his home in Buenos Aires to teach on a literacy programme being launched in Peru, led by Alicia Saco and sponsored by Peru's then revolutionary government. This literacy programme was known as ALFIN and its primary objective was to eliminate illiteracy from Peru. It was believed, at that time, that roughly 35 per cent of the 14 million people in Peru were illiterate. Boal, aware of Freire and his work and sharing his political stance towards the links between poverty and illiteracy, language and power, began to consider ways in which the language of theatre could be the means of offering liberatory education to the masses.

We are used to thinking of illiteracy meaning primarily the inability to read and write. Boal recognised and stated that the situation for illiterate adults in Peru was further complicated by the vast number of both languages and dialects spoken. He cited, as an example, the least-populated province in the country, Loreto, where there were forty-five different languages, not counting dialects. You will appreciate that illiterate adults in Peru needed to become able to express themselves not only in the official language of Spanish but also in their own first languages. This applies also in developed countries where there may be a host or official language which must be used to be accepted as a participative member of the community but where, in addition, many of the people struggle to maintain their first or home languages and dialects in order to retain their cultural identity and links with their past.

The ALFIN programme had two clear goals:

- To teach literacy in both first language and Spanish without forcing the abandonment of the former in favour of the latter.
- To teach literacy in all possible languages (where the word 'language' is used in the sense of Malaguzzi's hundred languages – especially the artistic languages of theatre, art, music, dance, photography, puppetry, films and journalism).

The intersection between the work of Paulo Freire and the world of early childhood development

At this point you are invited to draw on both your own experience and your reading so far. Politicians in the UK are currently making noises about how important it is for everyone in this country to speak English. It has even been suggested that parents speaking languages other than English ignore these and speak to their children only in English. This was the appalling advice given to my grandparents when they emigrated from Eastern Europe to South Africa. You may well know that this flies in the face of much research (see Baker 2001, Cummins 2001, Krashen 2004 and more) which shows just how important it is emotionally and cognitively for learners to be able to use both their first and subsequent languages.

It was essential to the success of the ALFIN literacy programme that the teachers were all selected to come from the same regions as the literacy students. This ensured some common themes in terms of dialect, experience and society. The training of these teachers was designed to follow four stages according to the special characteristics of each social group which were:

1) those from the slum areas,
2) those from rural areas,
3) those from mining areas, and
4) those from areas where Spanish was not the first language.

This was to ensure that the issues leading to the key concerns and vocabulary of each group could more easily be identified. You may remember reading earlier in this book some of the examples used as starting points for identifying generative words.

It was Boal's involvement in this teaching of adult literacy which led him to begin to think about how theatre could be used as a teaching tool – teaching for liberation. According to Boal the identification of issues key to the daily lives of the learners, together with the use of as many languages of as many types as possible, that became what he called the theatre strand of ALFIN. It is here that the participants *learn to speak and then read and write theatre.*

The dialogic approach in the theatre

So we know that Boal wanted to ensure that adult illiterate learners were enabled to use their awareness of what oppressed them in their lives and to challenge this in some way through making theatre. There is a clear difference in his developing philosophy between theatre that involves professional writers and actors and producers putting on a play with a political meaning from which the audience can 'learn' to requiring the audience to become the performers. Here the participants need to learn to *speak theatre* for themselves rather than passively watch plays written and performed in front of them. Boal's plan for transforming the spectator into actor followed four stages:

First the participants had to learn to *know their own bodies.* They need to discover what their bodies could do, what their bodies could not do, what could be changed and what not. To enable them to do this participants were introduced to a set of exercises or activities designed to enable them to come to know the range of what was possible purely through the use of the body. Many aspects of lifestyle affect the ways in which the body is used. Think about how the work that one does can define this. For example, someone who types sits at a desk and movement is limited to the slight movements of the upper body, much exercise of the hands and fingers and little more. A miner, by contrast, uses the whole body, often in difficult physical conditions, flexing muscles and limbs to carry and dig and move in small spaces. Those involved with the theatre must appreciate how people's daily lives often determine how they present themselves – how they stand and walk, greet people, exchange looks with one another and so on. To get the participants more able to use their bodies sensitively, they may have to unlearn some of the habits of their normal lives. To be actors they need to be able to analyse their own movements and change them. This is the start of being able to physically interpret and portray characters different from themselves.

Next they need to know *what their bodies can express*. Many cultures are very dependent on the spoken word to express feelings and ideas. A range of games was developed by ALFIN to encourage participants to use their bodies for such self-expression. One game was to give each participant a piece of paper on which was written the name of an animal. Each person then had to give a bodily impression of the named animal. Sounds and noises were not permitted. The fun part of the game was that each piece of paper also stated the gender of the named animal. During the game the aim was for the animals to recognise their 'mates' and leave the stage with them.

The third stage is what Boal called the *theatre as language*. If you are particularly interested in this you can read more about it in Boal (1979, 2000). It is difficult to understand fully exactly what is meant by this term, possibly because we are reading Boal's words in translation. We all recognise that language encompasses many aspects of communication. Theatre is very obviously about communication and in the best theatre you might encounter sets and props to contextualise the piece; music to add meaning and emotion; words and gesture and expression and body language to explain; movement and dance to enhance. This is made clear in Boal's Chart of Various Languages offered below.

Table 9.1 Boal's Chart of Various Languages

Communication of reality	Substantiation of reality	Transformation of reality
Spoken or written	Words	Built into sentences
Music	Instruments and the sounds they make (timbre, tones, notes and more)	Musical phrase made of melody and rhythm
Painting	Colours and forms	Each has its own syntax
Cinema	Image (secondarily music and speech)	Montage which involves splicing, superimposition, usage of lens, fade in and out and more.
Theater	Sum of all imaginable languages: words, colours, forms, movements, sounds, etc.	Dramatic action

(Boal 2000: 156)

The theatre that Boal developed became known as *forum theatre* and you can see many examples of it throughout the world. It starts with an issue, usually one concerned with oppression, and which has been selected and agreed by the group of those involved in the theatre. They then work collaboratively moving from being spectators to being active participants.

The process might look something like this: a question is raised and a solution offered: the participants either agree with it or disagree. Some of the participants become actors and perform a scene illustrating one point of view. Throughout this everyone is free to argue, discuss, keep up a dialogue until agreement is reached.

The final stage in Boal's analysis is *theatre as discourse*. Discourse can be defined in many ways but Boal used the term in the way in which Foucault did. Foucault was a French philosopher and social historian who said that discourse is the patterns of language that tell us more than what words alone might imply. What we hear or read allows us to analyse, for example what culture the person using the language is part of, what network of social institutions she is involved with and possibly even the basic assumptions she holds. Foucault (1994) said that discourse operates in four ways:

- It can be thought of as creating a world, a virtual world, very like the world of the theatre, which we construct through our complex inter-actions with one another, and between our experience, education and background. So discourse, in the form of the chains of language that bind us to others, *plays a key role in the social construction of reality*.
- It *can generate both knowledge and truth*. Knowledge is not just com-municated through language: it is constructed by us and organised through language itself.
- It *tells us about the people who speak and write it*. In literature the author invents the characters and puts words and thoughts in their mouths and minds and these allow the reader to deduce the history and culture of each character. In the theatre the people speaking it are not being themselves but taking on the roles of others – which implies adopt-ing the histories and cultures and positions in society of these others.
- It is *intimately involved with socially embedded networks of power*. In the theatre such issues of power can be examined, explored and chal-lenged. I was fortunate to see an excellent example of this in London in 2013 when the Young Vic Theatre Company – a very long way from Boal or Freire or Argentina or Brazil – produced a play called *A Season in the Congo*. The play was written by the black West Indian writer, Aime Cesaire, and it critically assessed the impact of Western imperial-ism and the devastating effects of the so-called civilising mission of the Belgian colonisers on the Congolese people. Along with the rest of the

audience, I was transported to a bar in the Congo where we witnessed the evocation of oppression by one group on another. The production included acting, singing, dance, movement, puppets, spoken languages, myth, lighting and design. It sold out to audiences of young and old people, all moved to laugh and weep at what was revealed to them about courage, betrayal, self-sacrifice, human dignity and the abuse of power. This is what Boal might call revolutionary theatre and its links back to Freire are simple to trace.

Freire, Boal and popular culture

Today, in much of the developing world, the ideals and ideas of Freire and Boal are used in theatres, bars, on street corners, in parks, in schools and village halls, in squares and on beaches, under trees and in marketplaces. Wherever we find ordinary people addressing the issues that concern them in myriad ways we can identify much of what Freire and Boal were concerned with. Anywhere that issues are discussed, explored, enacted, argued about, challenged and sometimes resolved can be described as the site of revolutionary theatre. The ways in which the resolution comes about very often involve what we might call popular culture.

Gramsci (discussed earlier in this book) examined how the dominant classes manage to retain their control over those 'beneath' them in the social structures. He used the word *hegemony* to describe the processes by which influential groups impose their power on others and maintain their hold once it has been established. The class holding power does not need to use coercion or brute force, but finds more subtle ways of imposing a set of ideas, values, principles, beliefs, objectives, cultural and political meanings. In other words when those in power decide that the people need to be persuaded of certain things in order that they support and do not oppose them (like austerity throughout much of Europe at the present time) the persuasion comes partially through popular culture. Think particularly about the American electoral process and how much importance is attached to celebrity support, image, dress, the adoption of key songs and so on.

But popular culture can equally act in the opposite direction. It can become the medium for helping those subject to powerful forces from above to resist. A famous case in point is what happened in Chile in Latin America where a strong and popular music developed from folk songs and where the singers were strongly opposed to the forces being massed against the people. The songs they wrote and sang became popular and powerful forces against the government – so powerful, in fact, that some of the singers – like Victor

Jara – were jailed and subsequently killed. In apartheid South Africa, too, music became an extremely powerful influence in the fight against apartheid.

In many examples of political theatre today you will find aspects of popular culture being used to oppose rather than accept domination. You can find parallels with the culture circles set up by Freire in his early attempts to address the issue of illiteracy.

Looking back, looking ahead

In this chapter we have examined the work of Augusto Boal who was deeply influenced by the work of Paulo Freire and applied it to the theatre, which was his area of expertise and passion. Boal became influential in his own right and much of what he tried and described has travelled throughout the world and continues to influence people in both the developed and the developing worlds.

In the final chapter we turn our attention to examples of learning in informal settings, some specifically Freirean and others not.

Chapter 10

No more silence

Learning in informal settings

In this, the last chapter of this book, we examine one explicitly Freirean example of teaching illiterate adults, looking at the book written by Victoria Purcell-Gates and Robin Waterman (2000) where they describe their own eighteen-month *ethnographic* study of a small group of women in El Salvador. The book is called *Now We Read, We See, We Speak*. From that we move on to examining the work of teachers in complementary classes in the city of Bradford which does not even mention Freire or acknowledge his influence. I can find it and I wonder if you can too.

Case study 1: how the Papaturro project came about

Victoria Purcell-Gates, a university-based researcher, had written a book called *Other People's Words* and in the process of writing that book had encountered the work of Freire. She was working in the USA and although she was influenced by much of what Freire said, she objected to what she called his Marxist tone when he talked of such things as oppressors, revolutionary change and liberation, thinking such terms were not appropriate to the USA. By the time she came to the end of the project described here she talked of herself as being as much of a political worker as a literacy teacher.

Robin Waterman had studied anthropology as an undergraduate both in the USA and Mexico. She later moved on to studying for a master's degree in education. She was very drawn to the writings of Freire when she started working as director of a community-based family literacy programme in Denver which was then a rather conservative city. The work of Freire was not well known and thought to have little application to those living in the USA but Waterman began to see how it might be both possible and useful to apply some of Freire's ideas. When she went to work and live in El Salvador and began her work with illiterate adults there her thinking turned to the work of Freire. She had long seen the political and social consequences of poverty and illiteracy and shared, with Freire, a conviction that literacy requires reading and speaking and writing not just the word but the world.

The project was designed to be ethnographic. The focus of the research was to be on a group of people sharing a culture. A researcher – in this case Robin – was to spend a long time observing and recording what she saw and heard. This was to be, by definition, an in-depth study, where Robin (an outsider in terms of culture) was to be actively involved in the project. She would record and teach but also interact as though she were a full and equal partner in the activities of the group. In other words, she was to adopt a dialogic approach. In more traditional research the researcher is expected to be apart from the research and to remain objective throughout. Ethnographic research, by its very nature, cannot require *objectivity*.

A note of warning, however. The study involved a very small sample – only eight Salvadorean women aged between twenty-three and sixty-six and they were learning to read and write for the first time in their lives. They were only eight out of the more than 800 million adults throughout the world who were at that time functionally illiterate and hence not full participating members of their communities. A small sample, studied over eighteen months, using the dialogic approach in an attempt to help move these women out of silence.

Meet the women

The eight women who began the study known as the Papaturro women's literacy class began as virtually illiterate, feeling blind and mute and vulnerable. At the end of the eighteen-month research phase they emerged as literate, active members of their communities. Let's have a taste of where they started and where they ended. Each individual's progress was analysed in terms of the difficulties she had and how she managed to overcome these.

- Deonicia was almost seventy years old when the project started. She could not write her name. She suffered from ill health but was so determined to learn that she did not miss a single session. She had great difficulty in understanding the differences between a syllable, a word and a sentence and, as a consequence, she tended to make slower progress than the other women. Robin paired her with Tomasa, her daughter-in-law, and this peer support enabled her to make more progress. By the end of the project Deonicia could read and write simple texts. She could talk critically about a range of issues that impacted on her life.

- Tomasa, Deonicia's daughter-in-law, had not gone to school. She had remained at home helping her mother. She had, however, attended a literacy class for roughly a year when she was in a refugee camp and she was able to write her own name and a few other simple words. She was described as being a self-directed learner and quickly became able to use letters in her own combinations to write words and sentences. She asked for extra work to do at home and began to initiate reading and writing events outside of the class. She began writing to her son in the USA. Like her mother-in-law, Tomasa knew stories from the Bible. She was able to develop some of the themes raised in the group as in this example: ' . . . we must struggle very hard so that the government fulfils its word and not let it be forgotten'. By the end of the study she was reading stories aloud to her children and literacy was being incorporated into the fabric of her daily life.
- Francisca suffered from poor health and poor eyesight. She regularly attended the classes and worked hard, particularly in contributing to the discussion of generative themes. (Remember them?) Her commitment to the class was so powerful that she even attended after being knocked down and trampled by a bull.
- Chunga, aged sixty-six, had had to leave primary school after only a few weeks. She, like Tomasa, had attended a literacy class whilst in refugee camps where she had acquired many literacy skills. She could write, but had not learned anything about the need for spaces between words and had developed her own idiosyncratic spelling rules. By the end of the project she was a thoughtful and articulate reader and writer.
- Celia was the most politically aware and critical member of the group. She often raised the themes of poverty, class and gender inequalities in class discussion and tried to write about these in her work. When Robin asked the women to read silently from one of their books Celia did not leave when the class ended but stayed behind to finish the story, at which point she wanted to talk about what she had read. Not surprisingly her growing literacy skills led to further and more intense community involvement.
- Margarita worked very hard and diligently but she did not achieve as much as some of the other women, possibly because she had responsibilities as a single parent and for her ailing mother. The question of dyslexia was raised. With peer support she was able, by the end of the project, to read back simple sentences she herself had written and to engage in group discussions.
- Carmelita was not able to attend regularly and suffered from ill health. She was shy and reticent and Robin feared that she had learning difficulties. With the support of the teacher and her peers she was able to read and write well enough to function effectively and to engage with her young children around literacy.

- Esperanza had had some early schooling in refugee camps and at home but she lacked confidence. Despite her poor attendance she succeeded in aspects of the programme and by the end had begun to use her literacy skills widely. She wrote to friends abroad and was able to read.

In line with much of life in Central America the Church plays a very dominant role in the everyday realities of the people and some would argue that it also plays some part in the oppression of the poor in society. When the women in the study began to be able to read, much of what they read came from the Bible.

The lives of the women: the generative themes

The women involved in the study had all suffered from poverty and oppression during their lives. Living in El Salvador in Central America, the smallest and most densely populated country on the continent, they had experienced extreme poverty living as campesinos working on the land. This is how Tomasa described her childhood.

> When I was born, we were very poor. Our house was very small. My father died soon after I was born and my mother was always looking for even small amounts of corn so that we could eat (there were six children). We ate tortillas with salt. Sometimes when she was able to get a bit of beans, we would eat beans. Sometimes she couldn't even find corn, so we didn't even have tortillas; we just endured the hunger. (Purcell-Gates and Waterman 2000: 27)

So poverty was endemic and so, too, was lack of health care. Celia described her experience when her firstborn baby, born when she was only seventeen, died.

> My baby, he died 8 days after I left for the hospital, dying of the same fever that I had. But my husband, he didn't always have the strength or capacity to tell me. He came every week to visit me, always telling me the baby was fine . . . But he was deceiving me. I cried every day in the hospital, crying for my baby. My milk was coming, and I kept forcing it out so that when I returned I could feed my baby. But he was already dead. (Ibid.: 27)

There was little or no access to education and where there were schools and the families were asked to send the children to school many were not able to do so because the children were needed to help in the home.

From this tiny portrait you begin to get a sense of just how many issues of oppression were present in the lives of these women and millions of other women and men, young and old, throughout the world.

One day in the literacy class

Robin begins the class with the generative word *tierra* which means land and which she has taken from the 'Facilitator's Manual' (written by the NGO Alfalit). She displays a poster of a peasant or campesino working on the land with the word TIERRA underneath. She then reads aloud to the class a piece from the manual about the ownership of land which raises many vital issues for the group. She then asks the group what the words they have heard have made them think of. This leads to a passionate sometimes historical and always personal set of responses from the women. Robin's role is to listen and intervene to affirm or question or move the discussion on.

Robin then invites the women to agree on one sentence that summarises all they have been saying. They agree on this and Robin writes it on the board and then the women, in chorus, read the sentence aloud three times. Following this the women copy the sentence into their own books and then write more of their thoughts. Robin reminds them that they should not worry about correct spelling or neat handwriting. What matters are their ideas. Robin goes round the group, one at a time, looking at and reading what they have written and then inviting them to read it aloud. They read what they have written first just to Robin but later aloud to the whole group. There is much nervous laughter about having to read aloud.

They now move on to learning the graphophonic code. As you may remember this from earlier in this book this is the analysis of the syllables: in this case the syllable families for the letters *n, l, m, b, s, r, rr* and *m* – so, for each initial letter the following pattern applies: *na-ne-ni-no-nu*.

Robin ends the session by focusing on what each student has achieved.

So we have seen how a typical day in this classroom operates on the whole-part-whole basis, with the class first involved in critical dialogue around serious and significant issues (the whole), then working on the smaller parts of reading and writing (letters, syllables, words, etc.) and then back to the whole where the teacher focuses on progress and builds self-esteem.

For the women involved this project it was entirely successful. Women who had not been able to read and write or participate in their communities found their voices and improved the quality of their lives. But since this is a single and very small ethnographic study it is impossible to generalise from it. It follows that the conclusions reached by the authors of the book in the form of insights for adult education are interesting but possibly not widely able to be generalised. The authors point out that there has been little proper research into the effectiveness of the dialogic approach and firmly believe that incorporating the real lives, the home languages and the authentic literacy needs of adult students is essential, just as we might insist that in order to work with young children it is essential to know as much as possible about their home lives, languages, culture, interests, fears, likes and dislikes, previous experience and more. The emphasis placed on decoding worries me and I believe that, since reading the word, like reading the world, depends on making and sharing meaning, an approach which focuses on the smallest units of language moves the focus from the whole to the part. I can find no meaning in trying to decode a nonphonetic language like English or break into syllables languages with regular syllabic structures.

Case study 2: bilingual approaches to learning literacy in complementary Saturday classes

Jean Conteh is Senior Lecturer in Primary Education at the University of Leeds and chair of a voluntary organisation which promotes bilingual teaching and learning in Bradford. She is one of the editors of the book *Multilingual Learning: Stories from Schools and Communities in Britain* (2007). The case study that follows is taken from this book.

Being bilingual is certainly not the same as or even similar to being illiterate. But there are ways in which those having a first language other than the host language of the country where they are being educated may be marginalised, alienated and silenced just because they are not fluent speakers, readers or writers of the host language. But let's take a closer look at what it might mean to be denied the right to speak your mother tongue in school. Jim Cummins has spent his academic life arguing for the maintenance of mother tongue in schools. In his paper (2001) he says that children in schools in North America and Europe often receive the message that if they want to be accepted by the teachers and society they have to renounce their allegiance to home language and culture. This can have disastrous consequences for children and their families and it violates their right to a decent education and undermines the links and bonds between children and their family members – parents, grandparents and so on. Many bilingual children are being marginalised and silenced, just as illiterate adults are. In one sense they are well able to read, write and speak the world but not the word.

Jean Conteh has long been interested in bilingualism and influenced by the work of Cummins, Baker and Skutnabb-Kangas. She says that complementary schools in Bradford tried to make the links between complementary and mainstream learning explicit. Complementary schools are schools additional to mainstream schools, often provided at the request of local groups with a shared language or culture, run by voluntary organisations and often able to use school buildings out of hours. Their focus may be on offering specific language classes. In the example we will be looking at, the teachers, who were all qualified primary school teachers, chose to use the same approaches and strategies required in mainstream schools in these complementary classes. The aim of this particular group of complementary schools is to raise the competence of bilingual children in the mainstream curriculum to help them achieve well in the exams they take at the end of the stage of primary education. In other words they want to enable bilingual pupils to be as successful as monolingual pupils in maths and English and science and more. And they base this on their awareness of the work of Cummins and others.

What research tells us about mother tongue development

Cummins cites some of these research findings in his paper (op. cit.). They are summarised here:

- If young children are allowed to develop their first languages throughout the primary school years they understand more about language itself and how to use it effectively. And when they develop literacy in more than one language they are able to compare and contrast how the two languages organise and reflect reality.
- Children who come to school with a solid foundation in their mother tongue develop stronger literacy abilities in the host language. And when parents and grandparents and carers are able to spend time with children reading or telling stories, singing songs, cooking or playing in the first language, children develop a wider vocabulary and set of skills and concepts in the home language. All this helps them be ready to tackle a new language and new set of concepts and skills.
- Maintaining mother tongue helps children develop not only mother tongue but also cognitive skills which help children perform well in school in all the traditional mainstream subjects.
- Spending teaching time on using more than one language does not hurt the academic development of anybody. Mother-tongue speakers feel accepted and valued. Monolingual children learn something about how other languages work. The *Foyer Project* in Belgium develops children's spoken and literacy abilities in three languages (whichever is their mother tongue, Dutch and French) throughout the primary school and

is proving to offer one of the best examples of the benefits of bilingual or trilingual education.

- Mother tongue use is fragile and easily lost. With its loss there is a loss of identity and culture and the risk of the loss of strong familial links. So rejecting a child's language is tantamount to rejecting the child.

The background in terms of language, cultural awareness and a bilingual approach

Conteh describes the first meeting on a cold March morning in Bradford. About forty adults and children gathered in a classroom in a small inner-city school to learn through using as many of the languages spoken by the group of students present to consider the subjects of the primary school curriculum. The adults present included some international students who had been invited to see just such classes where the teachers were using what they called a bilingual approach to learning. But most of the group was made up of the local children who turn up every Saturday morning for their regular bilingual complementary class which they have been attending for about six months.

Remember that teachers and children were all bilingual or multilingual. The range of languages was wide and included English, Punjabi, Hinko (a dialect of Punjabi), Urdu and Bangla (also known as Bengali) as the main languages, but also Mandarin, Taiwanese, Malay, Gujerati and perhaps one or two other languages. What came out of this was a lively two-hour session consisting of activities based around language awareness and learning about language carried out in the rich context of the linguistic and cultural diversity of the group involved.

Here we have the beginning of a project where a group of adults has decided to share their experience with children from their cultures in order to use one of the most vital of cultural tools – language – to enhance the life chances of the learners. The adults here are taking the initiative after noticing something which is disadvantaging certain children in the wider society. They have noticed that bilingual children do not do as well in mainstream schooling as many of their peers and feel that the presence of languages other than the host language may be the cause. Mainstream culture is preventing the children using their home languages in school.

During the morning the group learned to count in Chinese, Malay and Urdu and how to write their names in the three different scripts. They listened to an Urdu poem or *naath* which follows a rigidly defined syllabic pattern. This was chanted by a nine-year-old girl who had acquired her Urdu literacy at home from her mother. As the morning progressed it became difficult to know who were teachers and who were learners. The children were sometimes the experts who taught the adults as each group took on the role of teacher or learner. Conteh cites one example where one student wrote the name of his country, Negara Brunei Darussalam, on the board in Arabic script and told the children that it meant 'State of Brunei, abode of peace'. Ibraham, who had been born in Malawi into a Gujerati-speaking family and then moved to England at the age of fourteen, was amazed to hear the name and was able to link it with childhood memories of East Africa and Swahili. Humah, who had read the poem, identified some links with her language of Urdu and went on to write the name of Ali's village in Urdu. I am certain that you recognise this as a dialogic process.

The intersection between the work of Paulo Freire and the world of early childhood development

What makes this case study particular is that all the teachers, as well as all the children, were bilingual or, in some cases, multilingual. The teachers were able to use a range of languages in their teaching, with the aim of fulfilling the potential of each child by allowing them to use and build on what they already know. Those working with young children will recognise this as a fundamental factor. Good early childhood practitioners take time and trouble to find out what young children already know and can do. New learning can build on this solid foundation.

The bilingual teachers

The three teachers who run the complementary classes are members of local South-Asian heritage communities who have been settled in Bradford over more than two generations. All went to school in the UK and all work as teachers. Their own life experience has exposed them to racism, prejudice and aspects of alienation and this allows them to identify with learners today. They are all deeply committed to allowing the children to use their own languages whenever they want or need to and often this is based in their own experience where their particular linguistic skills have led either to praise or to negative judgements. Their teaching in the complementary classes is very similar to their teaching in mainstream, other than that they try to ensure that it is more dialogic and involves translation. This combination of participation and use of relevant languages is one way in which meanings can be amplified or opened up for all the children. They encourage the children to switch from language to language believing that such code-switching is a distinctive feature of being bilingual.

There is a fascinating example of how one of the teachers interacts with children during the playing of a maths game. This is too difficult to replicate but you can find it in Conteh's chapter (129–31). The teacher, Saiqa, wanted to develop the children's confidence in Punjabi and to this end she modelled a number of sentence structures in Punjabi. The children involved in the game were not all native Punjabi speakers. Here the interaction was teacher-led but the analysis of the session showed that each child spoke, seemed to be attentive and engaged. There was a lot of code-switching and examples of amplification, as described above.

The impact of Freire – explicit or implicit?

The influence of Freire is explicit in the first case study where Robin, the teacher, had specifically followed the models of dialogic teaching offered by Freire. Robin was determined that the topics for each session should be directly relevant to the lives of the group members. This did not mean that she allowed them the time in the group to come up with a pressing concern. Rather she used the 'Facilitator's Manual' to choose from. She then followed the structure devised by Freire of focusing on working on syllables in order to address literacy.

The second case study makes no reference to Freire and is, of course, not about teaching illiterate adults but about teaching bilingual children. But there are glimpses of Freire in the work. Conteh herself is deeply rooted in working with bilingual communities. Her communities are not made up of rural peasants but of urban families living in Bradford. She knows the communities, works in and with them and understands their concerns about the educational possibilities for their bilingual children. So, I would argue, there is a strong political foundation to her work, just as there was in Freire's. Her oppressed group is much less obviously oppressed, but nonetheless subject to lack of equal access to future success. And it is clear that the teaching that takes place is dialogic with everyone having a voice, being respected and acknowledged as they, together, teach and learn.

Looking back, looking ahead

In this last chapter we have looked at two case studies – one directly Freirean and the other not. In each case the spirit Freire is evident – the pressing and overriding need to take on the concerns of people denied access to full educational opportunities.

A final word

My area of expertise is the world of early childhood and until now I have not written about anything else. I did, of course, know of the work of Paulo Freire and had been privileged to hear him speak decades ago. In writing this book I have come to see more clearly the things that all marginalised people have in common and to pay tribute to those who have worked to deal seriously with redressing aspects of the status quo. When Freire died in 1997 tributes were paid from individuals and organisations throughout the world. He had collaborated with UNESCO and received many prizes including the 1996 UNESCO prize for Peace Education. The director of UNESCO said this of him:

> A pioneer in the fight against illiteracy, Paulo Freire demonstrated – more than anyone – that education was the foundation of all freedoms; that it alone can give people mastery over their destiny . . . His life – which did not spare him from either prison or exile – was a reflection of his doctrine: the practice of freedom. He who has left us was a giant of the spirit and heart. He will be both an example and a fertile source of inspiration for future generations. (www.ipsnews.net/1997/05/united-nations-unescos-tribute-to-paulo-freire/)

And Moacir Gadotti, mentioned in this book and author of a very personal book on Freire, wrote this:

> What does an educator leave as a legacy? In the first place he leaves a life, a biography. And Paulo enchanted us with his gentleness, his mildness, his charisma, his consistency, his commitment, his seriousness. His words and actions were words and actions of struggle for a 'less ugly, less wicked, less inhuman' world, as he used to say. Along with love and hope, he also leaves us a legacy of indignation in the face of injustice. (http://waccglobal.org/en/19973-indigenous-communications/922-The-political-pedagogical-praxis-of-Paulo-Freire-1921–97-Dreaming-of-a-world-of-equality-and-justice–.html)

Freire's work has been translated into many languages and one can find evidence of his thinking in the developed and developing worlds, in schools and settings and universities, colleges and informal classes, in work with young people and older people. I have learned a great deal about Freire and his principles and have sometimes struggled to represent clearly my interpretation of what he was saying. And I have come to consider him truly one of the great figures in both in education and liberation.

To end with, here is a quote from Cornel West's tribute in the preface to *Paulo Freire: A Critical Encounter*:

> Freire's genius is to explicate . . . and exemplify . . . the dynamics of this process of how ordinary people can and do make history in how they think, feel, act and love. Freire has the distinctive talent of being a profound theorist who remains 'on the ground' and a passionate activist who gets us 'off the ground' – that is, he makes what is abstract concrete without sacrificing subtlety, and he infuses this concrete way of being-in-the-world with a fire that fans and fuels our will to be free. (McLaren and Leonard 1993: xiii)

Glossary

addressivity A term used by Bakhtin in connection with language. It refers to any human being's capacity to engage in communication for the sake of the other partner or partners.

alienation The process by which individuals or groups are made to feel that they don't belong, have no stake in anything and are silenced.

alphabetizer The person who collects the words used by different communities, using a notebook or a tape recorder. This takes place in the first stage of the culture circle programmes.

authoritarianism It is usually used to describe a form of government but its wider meaning implies unquestioning obedience to authority, as against individual freedom and related to the expectation of unquestioning obedience.

banking education One of Freire's key terms where he compares a style of teaching to what happens in banks: information is banked in the empty head of the learner. The passive learner is being filled with knowledge.

beings of praxis Freire borrowed this phrase from Marx and used it to describe a characteristic of being human. What it means is that humans, unlike animals, think about and transform aspects of the world.

capacity building A term common in South Africa used to describe attempts to better the lives of the poor and oppressed but where the attempts are not in relation to the issues or questions raised by these people but others trying to do good in their names.

code-switching Bilingual and multilingual people are able to move from one language or dialect to another with ease and do it to increase comprehension.

codifications Another item in Freire's programme for countering illiteracy was presenting the ideas that emerged in the initial session of finding generative words as some sort of image. For him these were codifications.

commodity Something that can be bought.

competency This means ability.

complementary school These are schools other than mainstream schools, often offering special classes to speakers of other languages.

conscientization The process of being conscious particularly about what is wrong and thus having the power to change it.

consciousness Means an awareness of. To be conscious is to understand and know. In one sense it is used to indicate our understanding that we are separate from but involved in the world.

creative powers The ability to ask questions and find new ways of changing the unacceptable or making something new and unique.

critical activist Someone who asks questions and acts on the answers. The term 'militant' was used to mean the same thing in a South African context.

critical reader Someone who reads for meaning and is able to assess the quality or importance or impact of what is being read.

cultural imperialism This refers to the effects of one powerful group exerting influence over other groups. The only acceptable culture is that of the rich and powerful. It is one of the ways of keeping groups and individuals silent and voiceless.

cultural politics Where dominance and subordination are both defined and contested. An example could be a school or a meeting or a hospital or any place where some people are expected to be kept in their place.

cultural tools These are the things made by human beings in groups to enable them to express their feelings and solve their problems. They include physical tools like pencils and spades, but also abstract things like numbers.

culture circle Freire organised for groups of people to gather together in small groups as part of his complicated programme of teaching literacy. These were known as culture circles.

culture of silence Those exposed to an educational system that doesn't invite them to raise questions learn to remain silent. The education system sets up and maintains a culture of silence. This means that they accept their plight and do not even discuss it with one another.

decodification This is the process where those involved in creating codifications begin to be able to see themselves in the image itself and able to critically review the image which has been drawn from their own realities.

dialect A form of language closely related to place or class or group.

dialogic A key term for Freire relating to how he believed people could learn from one another. Dialogic relationships are between equals and in education this means that the teacher and student show one another mutual respect and their exchanges are in the form of dialogue.

dialogic talk   Robin Alexander's term to describe talk where both teachers and pupils make contributions which help the learners move forward.

dialogue   A conversation or exchange between two or more people on the basis of equality. Freire contrasted it with anti-dialogue which he saw as the handing down of information in an unequal exchange.

dirty list   A list introduced in Brazil in 2005 to keep track of companies employing people to work for slave wages and terrible working conditions.

discourse   The patterns of language that reveal more than what is just in the words.

domesticating literacy   Close to functional literacy but used to describe the level of reading and writing which allow people to stay where they are in society. In other words a literacy which does not invite or allow for questioning.

domestication   Education for domestication is education which maintains the status quo. Some argue that in this type of education learners suffer from some form of mental abuse which keeps them mute.

emancipatory   To emancipate is to rescue someone from something. Emancipatory means doing this. For Freire literacy could and should be emancipatory.

ethnographic   A word used to describe the kind of research which takes place in the real-life place to which the research is related. It may be in people's homes, in classrooms, in work places.

exploited   Where advantage is taken of one group by another. It is a form of oppression.

forum theatre   Theatre which starts with an issue, often related to the oppressed, and then developed and produced collaboratively and dialogically.

functional literacy   The ability to read and write at a minimal level in order to be able to function within society.

generative words   In the first phase of Freire's literacy programme it was the identification of these words which were seen to be of common significance to members of the group and capable of being broken down into constituent syllables which could then be used to generate new words.

graphic systems   Writing systems – including alphabets and scripts and more.

hegemony   A term most closely associated with Gramsci and meaning the predominance of one group or class over another. It can suggest not only power and economic control but also the ability of those with the power to keep those without silent.

human sense   Something makes human sense when its purpose is clear. You may question whether breaking words down into syllables in order to recombine these to make new words makes human sense.

humanising The effect of making someone feel more worthwhile and respected and human.

informal or popular Centres of teaching and learning not part of mainstream schools or colleges.

internalised In connection with language and thought, something that is obvious or explicit becomes hidden and implicit by the process of being internalised. You can no longer see or hear it but it is in your head.

Investigation Stage The first stage of the literacy programme for the culture circles during which the alphabetizer gathers words.

know own bodies What spectator actors have to do in order to convey meaning through movement and gesture.

knowledge production This is where knowledge is not reserved for the few but created by all those involved in a pedagogical context.

knowledge transmission Where, in traditional classrooms and settings, the teacher holds the knowledge and passes it on to the learners. The essence of banking education.

knowledgeable equals Freire phrase to show his insistence that all partners in any dialogue are equals and have knowledge gained from their experience and their culture.

liberating literacy (or education) Also called critical literacy, racial literacy or transformative literacy. The ability to understand and to question, not only to name and recite. People taught to read by focusing on the small units are able to decode and say aloud. People taught to read in order to find and sometimes challenge the meaning are engaged in liberating literacy.

literacy Everything to do with the written word. Adult literacy refers primarily to helping those who have not learned to read and write to do so. For Gramsci literacy is both a social construct (made by human beings) and a social practice (carried out by human beings). It is also a radical construct which means that it has the possibility of having far-reaching effects. For Freire it was primarily seen as a tool to allow marginalised people to begin to be able to participate in society after learning to read and write the world.

lived experience A synonym for everyday life.

marginalised Individuals or groups who are marginalised are pushed to the edges of mainstream society, not accepted, recognised or valued. It is a form of oppression.

material conditions The physical and financial circumstances.

mediated by Something that allows change to take place.

naming (the world) Identifying, recognising, describing and reflecting on the people, events, objects in the world.

narrative nature   With regard to banking education, Freire talked of the narrative nature of the relationships between the teacher and learner. The term literally means 'story-like behaviour'.

neoliberalism   The term *neoliberal* is now used mainly by those who are critical of legislative market reforms such as free trade, deregulation, privatisation, and reducing government control of the economy.

objectification   Seeing or treating people as objects.

objectivity   Not taking sides but remaining open to being persuaded.

ontological   The essence of being human.

ontological vocation   The way in which human beings seek to achieve equality in their lives.

oppression   This is an everyday word used to describe what happens to people who are at the bottom of the human pile and subject to the whims, laws and actions of those with more money, power and social capital.

outreach programme   An education or other programme situated in the community.

overgeneralising   When children are acquiring their first language they move on from imitating what they hear to working out the rules and applying them to every situation. So they begin to make mistakes.

paradigms   These are old methods or ideas that are widely accepted.

paternalistic   Well-intentioned actions carried out by people who want to do good but not basically change society. Literally the word paternal means 'like a father'.

pedagogical situation   A teaching and learning situation.

peer teaching sessions   Where children teach one another.

phonemic   A phoneme is a basic unit of a language's phonology or sounds system which is combined with other phonemes to form meaningful units such as words or morphemes. So it can be described as 'the smallest contrastive linguistic unit which may bring about a change of meaning'.

popular culture   The culture of ordinary people, of the streets, of today.

popular thinking   The thinking of ordinary people.

praxis   Praxis means both action and reflection. Freire said that humans were unlike animals in that they both experience and reflect and act on their experience. He said humans were beings of praxis.

Problematization Stage   The final stage of Freire's pedagogy where the focus moves on to learning the skills of reading and writing.

problem-posings   Where the situation explicitly or implicitly invites participants to ask questions.

radical adult education   Education which seeks to help people not accept but challenge the status quo.

reading the world   A phrase coined by Freire and widely used in all his work, it refers to making sense of the physical, social, cultural, lived world. For Freire being able to do this had to precede learning to read the word.

recognition   Bruner defined it as the process of seeing something, comparing it with something else, spotting similarities and differences, putting it into a category – all in order to not only know what it is but also to know what it might be.

reinforce   When talking about behaviour and learning, reinforcement is what happens when an action of any kind receives a positive response. The effect is to make the learner more likely to repeat whatever it was that earned the positive response. Negative responses tend to make the leaner less likely to repeat the action.

responsivity   Bakhtin's term which explains how in dialogue the listener is not passive but responds in some way. The first speaker in turn then responds and so responsivity works in both directions.

schematic behaviour   Describes the behaviour of young children who show patterns of repetition – being interested in anything that goes round, or in carrying things from one place to another. An interest of Piaget.

situated learning   A model of learning in a community of practice. At its simplest, situated learning is learning that takes place in the same context in which it is applied.

social capital   For our purposes it means the links and shared values that people in groups develop as they work or learn together. It also means the benefits people have as they become better educated, more literate and more able to participate in society.

social class empowerment   The idea of ensuring that everyone in a social class is able to work together to emancipate themselves.

social construct   Something that has been made or created by people.

social movements   Where groups of people band together because they have a goal or an interest or a philosophy in common.

socialist   An economic system characterised by social ownership of the means of production and co-operative management of the economy.

sociocultural approach   Examine something in the light of culture, context and language.

sociolinguistic   Examine something in the light of context and culture and language.

speak theatre   In Boal's work to speak theatre is to actively participate in the creation of a play. The spectator becomes the actor.

specific dignity   The phrase used by Lenira Haddad in her criticism of what is happening in Brazil as attempts are made to deny early childhood its particular features and nature.

sustainable societies   Communities where aspects of life can be sustained, avoiding exploitation and ensuring that the effects of development maintain an ecological balance and minimize the depletion of natural resources.

syllabically   Portuguese is a richly syllabic language, like Italian and Spanish. This feature of the language allowed Freire to focus in his teaching of reading and writing on the syllable (to act syllabically) rather than on the phoneme.

talk descriptors   Ways of describing talk in classrooms which indicate that the situation is dialogic. They are collective, reciprocal, supportive, cumulative and purposeful. You will see descriptions in the text.

the world   Everything that takes place wherever any human being is.

theatre as language   In Boal's work to speak theatre is to actively participate in the creation of a play. The spectator becomes the actor.

Thematization Stage   This is the second stage of the literacy programme in the culture circles and involves codifying and decodifying.

two-way communication   Freire's term to describe that dialogue is always to and from each person involved. All those involved are both teachers and learners, speakers and listeners.

what bodies express   A way of not depending on spoken language alone to express feelings.

Bibliography

Note: There are often many editions of some of the books. I have cited the editions to which I have referred.

Ada, A. F. (1988) 'The Pajaro Valley experience' in Tove Skutnabb-Kangas and Jim Cummins (eds), *Minority Education: From Shame to Struggle*. Clevedon: Multilingual Matters.

A Language in Common (2000) QCA Publications.

Alexander, R. (2006) *Education as Dialogue: Moral and Pedagogical Choices for a Runaway World*. Hong Kong: Hong Kong Institute of Education with Dialogos.

Aronowitz, S. (2001) 'Introduction' in P. Freire, *Pedagogy of Freedom: Ethics, Democracy and Civic Courage*. London: Rowman & Littlefield Publishers.

Baker, C. (2001) *Foundations of Bilingual Education and Bilingualism*. Clevedon: Multilingual Matters.

Bakhtin, M. M. (1986) *Speech Genres and Other Late Essays*. Edited by Caryl Emerson and Michael Holquist. Translated by Vern W. McGee. Austin, TX: University of Texas Press.

Bissex, G. (1984) *GNYS AT WK: A Child Learns to Write and Read*. Cambridge, MA: Harvard University Press.

Boal, A. (1979, 2000) *Theater of the Oppressed*. London: Pluto Press.

Hall, B. L., Clover, D. E., Crowther, J. and Scandrett, E. (eds) (2012) *Learning and Education for a Better World: The Role of Social Movements*. Rotterdam, Boston, Taipei: Sense Publishers.

Castells, M., Flecha, R., Freire, P., Giroux, H. A., Macedo, D. and Willis, P. (1999) *Critical Education in the New Information Age*. Lanham, MD: Rowman & Littlefield Publishers.

Cole, M. (1996) *Cultural Psychology: A Once and Future Discipline*. Cambridge, MA: Harvard University Press.

Conteh, J. (2007) 'Culture, languages and learning: Mediating a bilingual approach in complementary Saturday class' in Jean Conteh, Peter Martin and Leena Helavaara Robertson (eds) (2007), *Multilingual Learnings: Stories from Schools and Communities in Britain*. Stoke on Trent: Trentham Books.

Conteh, J., Martin, P. and Robertson, L. H. (eds) (2007) *Multilingual Learnings: Stories from Schools and Communities in Britain*. Stoke on Trent: Trentham Books.

Cummins, J. (2001) 'Bilingual children's mother tongue: Why is it important for education?' *Sprogforum*, 7(19), 15–20. Available at www.iteachilearn.com/cummins/mother.htm

Elias, N. (1994) *The Established and the Outsiders: A Sociological Enquiry into Community Problems*. 2nd edn London: Sage Publications.

Fain, J. G. (2008) '"Um, they weren't thinking about their thinking": Children's talk about issues of oppression.' *Multicultural Perspectives*, 10(4), 201–8.

Figlan, L., Mavuso, M., Ngema, B., Nsibande, Z., Sibisi, S. and Zikode, S. (2009) *Living Learning*. Pietermaritzburg: Church Land Programme.

Figueiredo-Cowen, M. de and Gastaldo, D. (eds) (1995) *Paulo Freire at the Institute*. London: Institute of Education.

Foucault, M. (1994) *The Order of Things: An Archaeology of the Human Sciences*. London: Vintage Books.

Freire, A.M.A. and Macedo, D. (eds) (2001) *The Paulo Freire Reader*. New York and London: Continuum.

Freire, P. (1972) *Cultural Action for Freedom*. Harmondsworth: Penguin.

Freire, P. (1985) *The Politics of Education: Culture, Power and Liberation*. New York: Seabury Press.

Freire, P. (1993, 1996) *Pedagogy of the Oppressed*. London: Penguin Books.

Freire, P. (1994) *Pedagogy of Hope: Reliving Pedagogy of the Oppressed*. New York: Continuum.

Freire, P. (1998) *Teachers as Cultural Workers*. Boulder, CO: Westview Press.

Freire, P. (2001) *Pedagogy of Freedom: Ethics, Democracy and Civic Courage*. London: Rowman & Littlefield Publishers.

Freire, P. (2004a) *Pedagogy of Indignation*. Boulder, CO: Paradigm Publishers.

Freire, P. (2004b) *Pedagogy of Hope*. London and New York: Continuum.

Freire, P. (2005) *Education for Critical Consciousness*. London and New York: Continuum.

Freire, P. (2009) *Pedagogy of Hope*. London and New York: Continuum.

Freire, P. and Macedo, D. (1987) *Literacy: Reading the Word and the World*. London: Routledge and Kegan Paul.

Frymer, B. (2005) 'Freire, alienation, and contemporary youth: Toward pedagogy of everyday life.' *Interactions: UCLA Journal of Education and Information Studies*, 1(2), 1–16.

Gadotti, M. (1994) *Reading Paulo Freire: His Life and Work*. Albany, NY: State University of New York Press.

Gudschinsky, S. C. (1967) *How to Learn an Unwritten Language (Studies in Anthropological Method)*. New York: Holt, Rinehart and Winston.

Haddad, L. (2008) 'For a specific dignity of ECE: Policy and research issues relating to the education of young children and sustainable society' in Ingrid Pramling Samuelsson and Yoshie Kaga (eds), *The Contribution of Early Childhood Education to a Sustainable Society* (pp. 31–6). Paris: UNESCO. Available at www.oei.es/decada/unesco_infancia.pdf

Hall, S. (1982) 'The rediscovery of "ideology": Return of the repressed in media studies' in Michael Gurevitch, Tony Bennett, James Curran and Janet Woollacott (eds), *Culture, Society and the Media*. London: Methuen.

Harley, A. (2012) '"We are poor, not stupid": Learning from autonomous grass-roots social movements in South Africa' in Budd L. Hall, Darlene Clover, Jim Crowther and Eurig Scandrett (eds), *Learning and Education for a Better World: The Role of Social Movements* (pp. 3–22). Rotterdam: Sense Publishers.

Horton, M., Freire, P. and Bell, B. (eds) (1991) *We Make the Road by Walking: Conversations on Education and Social Change.* Philadelphia: Temple University Press.

Kenner, C. (2004) 'Community school pupils reinterpret their knowledge of Chinese and Arabic for primary school peers' in Eve Gregory, Susi Long and Dinah Volk (eds), *Many Pathways to Literacy: Young Children Learning with Siblings, Grandparents, Peers and Communities* (pp. 105–16). New York: Routledge Falmer.

Kozol, K. (1991) *Savage Inequalities: Children in America's Schools.* New York, NY: Harper Perennial.

Krashen, S. (2004) 'Defending whole language: The limits of phonics instruction and the efficacy of whole language instruction.' *Reading Improvement, 39*(1): 32–42.

Levi, P. (2005) *The Black Hole of Auschwitz.* Marco Belpoliti (ed.). Cambridge-Malden: Polity Press.

Levine, K. (1986) *The Social Context of Literacy.* London: Routledge and Kegan Paul.

McInerney, P. (2009) 'Toward a critical pedagogy of engagement for alienated youth: Insights from Freire and school-based research.' *Critical Studies in Education, 50*(1), 23–35.

McLaren, P. and Lankshear, C. (eds) (1994) *Politics of Liberation: Paths from Freire.* London: Routledge.

McLaren, P. and Leonard, P. (eds) (1993) *Paulo Freire: A Critical Encounter.* London: Routledge.

Mercer, N. (2003) 'The educational value of "dialogic talk" in "whole-class dialogue"' in *New Perspectives on Spoken English in the Classroom* (pp. 73–6). London: Qualifications and Curriculum Authority.

Mercer, N., Dawes, L. and Staarman, J.K. (2009) 'Dialogic teaching in the primary science classroom.' *Language and Education, 23*(4), 353–69.

Mercer, N. and Littleton, K. (2007) *Dialogue and the Development of Children's Thinking: A Sociocultural Approach.* London and New York: Routledge

Mortenson, G. (2010) *Stones into Schools: Promoting Peace with Books, not Bombs, in Afghanistan and Pakistan.* London: Penguin.

Paley, V.G. (1929) *Bad Guys Don't Have Birthdays.* Chicago: University of Chicago Press.

Paley, V.G. (1981) *Wally's Stories.* Cambridge, MA: Harvard University Press.

Papatheodorou, T. (2005) *Behaviour Problems in the Early Years: A Guide for Understanding and Support.* Abingdon and New York: RoutledgeFalmer.

Papatheodorou, T. and Moyles, J. (eds) (2005) *Cross-Cultural Perspectives on Early Childhood.* London: Sage Publications.

Patchett, A. (2008) *Run.* New York, NY: Harper Perennial.

Pea, R. D. (1993) 'Practices of distributed intelligence and designs for education' in G. Solomon (ed.), *Distributed Cognitions: Psychological and Educational Considerations* (pp. 47–87). Cambridge, MA: Cambridge University Press.

Purcell-Gates, V. and Waterman, R. A. (2000) *Now We Read, We See, We Speak: Portrait of Literacy Development in an Adult Freirean-Based Class*. Mahwah, NJ: Lawrence Erlbaum Associates.

Rabideau, D. (ed.) (1989) *El espanol en marcha [Spanish on the March]*. Comite de Educacion Basica en Espanol.

Shor, I. and Freire, P. (1986) *A Pedagogy for Liberation: Dialogues on Transforming Education*. Westport, CT: Bergin & Garvey.

Shor, I. and Freire, P. (1987) 'What is the "dialogical method" of teaching.' *Journal of Education, 169*(3), 11–31.

Skutnabb-Kangas, T. and Cummins, J. (eds) (1988) *Minority Education: From Shame to Struggle*. Clevedon: Multilingual Matters.

Smidt, S. (2009) *Introducing Vygotsky*. London and New York: Routledge.

Smidt, S. (2011) *Introducing Bruner*. London and New York: Routledge.

Smidt, S. (2013) *Introducing Malaguzzi*. London and New York: Routledge.

Statham, L. (ed.) (2008) *Counting Them In: Isolated Bilingual Learners in Schools*. Stoke on Trent: Trentham Books.

Sticht, T. G. and Armstrong, W. B. (1975) *Adult Functional Competency: A Summary*. Austin, TX: University of Texas Press.

Taylor, P. (1993) *The Texts of Paulo Freire*. Buckingham: Open University Press.

Touati, F. (1987) *Desperate Spring: Lives of Algerian Women*. Translated by Ros Schwartz. The Women's Press.

Vygotsky, L. S. (1962) *Thought and Language*. Edited and translated by E. Haufmann and G. Vakar. Cambridge, MA: MIT Press.

Index